Best Hikes Atlanta

HELP US KEEP THIS GUIDE UP TO DATE

Every effort has been made by the authors and editors to make this guide as accurate and useful as possible. However, many things can change after a guide is published—trails are rerouted, regulations change, techniques evolve, facilities come under new management, and so on.

We would appreciate hearing from you concerning your experiences with this guide and how you feel it could be improved and kept up to date. While we may not be able to respond to all comments and suggestions, we'll take them to heart, and we'll also make certain to share them with the authors. Please send your comments and suggestions to the following address:

FalconGuides
Reader Response/Editorial Department
246 Goose Lane, Suite 200
Guilford, CT 06437

Thanks for your input, and happy trails!

Best Hikes Atlanta

The Greatest Views, Wildlife, and Historic Sites

SECOND EDITION

Ren and Helen Davis

FALCONGUIDES

GUILFORD, CONNECTICUT

To our son, Nelson, his wife, Alyson, and grandsons Luke, Isaac, Caleb, and Daniel, as they walk through life together.

FALCONGUIDES®

An imprint of The Rowman & Littlefield Publishing Group, Inc.
4501 Forbes Blvd., Ste. 200
Lanham, MD 20706
www.rowman.com

Falcon and FalconGuides are registered trademarks and Make Adventure Your Story is a trademark of The Rowman & Littlefield Publishing Group, Inc.

Distributed by NATIONAL BOOK NETWORK

Photos by Ren and Helen Davis
Maps: © 2018 The Rowman & Littlefield Publishing Group, Inc.

British Library Cataloguing-in-Publication Information Available

Library of Congress Cataloguing-in-Publication Information available

ISBN 978-1-4930-3493-2 (paperback)
ISBN 978-1-4930-3494-9 (e-book)

∞™ The paper used in this publication meets the minimum requirements of American National Standard for Information Sciences—Permanence of Paper for Printed Library Materials, ANSI / NISO Z39.48-1992.

Printed in the United States of America

Contents

Overview

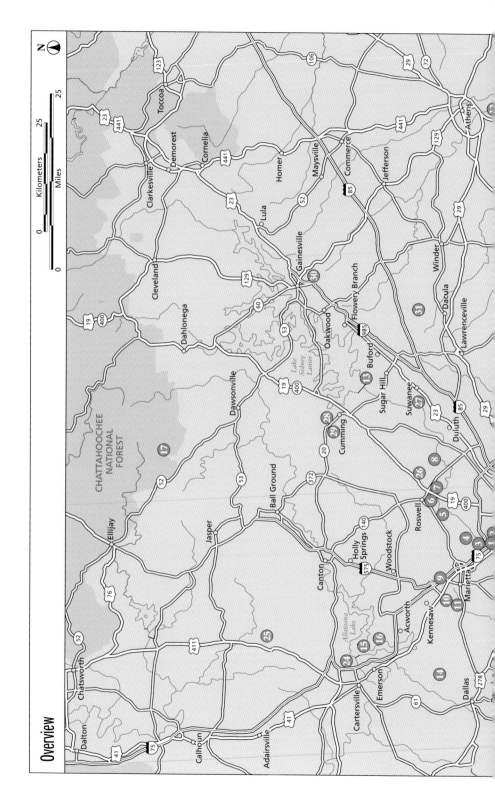

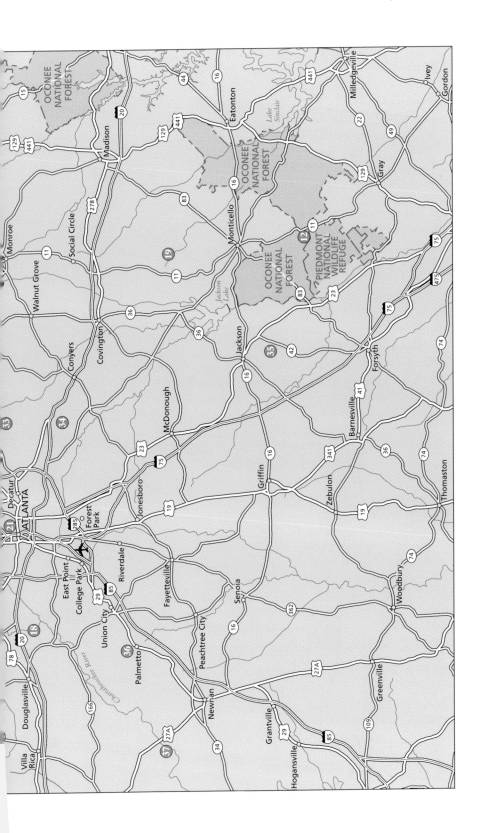

Local Parks and Gardens

Acknowledgments

We are grateful to the many individuals who shared both their love of the outdoors and their expertise with us as we hiked around the Atlanta area during the past year. Since penning our original walking guide to the area in 1988, it is always a delight to return to familiar places to see how they have changed (or not) and to discover new destinations to share. For us, this guide was a little bit of both. We extend our thanks to the following individuals for their help and guidance in preparing this book.

From the National Park Service, we received guidance from Bill Cox and Jerry Hightower of the Chattahoochee River National Recreation Area, and Retha Stephens from Kennesaw Mountain National Battlefield Park. From other federal agencies, we were guided by Michael Lapina of the US Army Corps of Engineers office at Lake Sidney Lanier for details about the Laurel Ridge Trail, and Andrew Hammond at the Piedmont National Wildlife Refuge.

Representatives from the Georgia Department of Natural Resources who provided assistance with trails include Kim Hatcher from Georgia State Parks, Don Scarborough of Sweetwater Creek State Park, Samantha Wiley at Red Top Mountain State Park, and Dillan Lee and Gary Ansorge of Pickett's Mill State Historic Site. In addition, Walter Lane and Linda May were generous with their help in reviewing information about the Charlie Elliott Wildlife Center.

Atlanta's local parks make up the majority of hiking destinations profiled in this guide, and we were fortunate to have enthusiastic help from many individuals who shared their expertise and offered assistance. From Georgia's Stone Mountain Park, we received help from Naomi Thompson; Ed McBrayer of the PATH Foundation provided guidance on the two chapters profiling sections of the Silver Comet Trail; and Ike English shared his excitement for the beauty of Dauset Trails. Laura Pate kept us updated on Sawnee Mountain Preserve; Cynthia Taylor provided information about Elachee Nature Science Center; Mera Cardenas did the same for Davidson-Arabia Mountain Nature Preserve. Darrell McCook shared insights on Piedmont Park, Lisa Kennedy helped with the State Botanical Garden of Georgia; Regina Wheeler confirmed details about the Pine Mountain Recreation Area and Pine Log Creek Trails. Finally, we were delighted to get help with the Suwanee Creek Greenway from Lynne DeWilde; assistance with information on Little Mulberry Park from Tammy Gibson; details from Mike Perry on the Big Creek Greenway; and support from Kimberly Barnett from Chattahoochee Hills for information on changes at Cochran Mill Park. Everyone with whom we worked shared our love of the outdoors and enthusiasm for encouraging others to discover it for themselves.

In closing, we want to thank John Burbidge, Ellen Urban, and all the Falcon-Guides staff who offered help, advice, guidance on myriad details, and ongoing support throughout this project.

Introduction

Atlanta has long been touted as "the city of trees," and despite explosive population growth (as of 2017 the population of metropolitan Atlanta was nearly six million), both within the city and its surrounding suburbs, Atlanta still offers many easily accessible woodlands, parks, and green spaces suitable for family outings or more rigorous treks. Wherever you are in Atlanta, there are destinations to suit your interest, from mountaintop vistas and paths along rushing streams to urban parkways great for a jog or bicycle ride and historic sites linking us to those who came before.

Atlanta is also blessed with a new generation of civic leaders and environmental advocates who continue to preserve green spaces and create new parks across the region. A growing number of these, like the BeltLine, Silver Comet, Suwanee Creek, and Big Creek Greenway Trails, are linear parks that meander through developed areas, offering residents and visitors opportunities for outdoor recreation close to work or home.

Old Grist Mill on Cherokee Trail by Stone Mountain Lake. See Hike 33.

For us, a walk in the woods has always been a way to escape the hectic pace of urban living and to recalibrate our lives to be more in synch with nature's rhythms. Because of its climate, vibrant city life, and its easy access to mountains, woodlands, and waterways, Atlanta has long been considered one of America's most livable cities. We hope that this guide may be a small contribution to sustaining that reputation into the future.

As Atlanta continues to grow and expand, its parks and trails will become increasingly important resources for urban residents and visitors seeking to reconnect with a natural world close to home.

Atlanta's Natural and Human History

Atlanta and the surrounding area are in the heart of the Southern Piedmont ("piedmont" means "foot of the mountain"), one of four distinct geological regions of Georgia. The others are the Ridge and Valley of northwestern Georgia, the Blue Ridge in northeastern Georgia, and the Coastal Plain, stretching southward to the Atlantic Ocean from the Fall Line that marks the boundary between the piedmont and the plain.

The piedmont is crisscrossed by a network of streams and rivers, most with their headwaters in the mountains, flowing toward the Atlantic or the Gulf of Mexico. For more than 10,000 years, these waterways and surrounding valleys served as migration and trade routes for ancient peoples moving southeastward and, more recently, for Euro-American settlers traveling from the coast into the interior. The result is a landscape that is both geologically complex and rich in human history.

Natural History

The Southern Piedmont, stretching northeast from Alabama through the Carolinas, is part of the larger Piedmont region that follows the eastern slopes of the Appalachian Mountains as far north as New York. In Georgia the piedmont landscape is characterized by low mountains and foothills in the north that gradually descend in elevation to the Fall Line, a distinctive geological boundary separating the harder crystalline rocks of the piedmont from the softer soils of the Coastal Plain. The Fall Line cities of Augusta, Macon, and Columbus were established at the navigational heads of the Savannah, Ocmulgee, and Chattahoochee Rivers, where they descended on cataracts from the piedmont hills.

The rocks underlying the piedmont are among the oldest and most tortured on earth. Created more than a billion years ago, the Precambrian Era stone, laid down as sediments, was later altered by heat and pressure into harder metamorphic rock. Over many hundreds of millions of years, this stone was faulted, folded, and uplifted during several periods of mountain building caused by drifting continents and dramatic climate changes. During the Ordovician Period (488 to 444 million years ago), the area was marked by extensive volcanic activity. Eruptions deposited massive amounts of ash that weathered to bentonite, the iron-rich, reddish clay soil that underlies much of northern Georgia.

A subsequent mountain-building era during the Pennsylvanian and Permian Periods (318 to 248 million years ago) was caused by the collision of the African, European, and North American continents to form the supercontinent of Pangaea. These collisions uplifted the ancient Appalachian Mountain Range to elevations higher than the current Himalayas. Under tremendous heat and pressure, some of the metamorphosed rocks far below the surface melted into large bodies of granite magma.

After Pangaea broke apart and the continents began to drift to their current locations, weathering dramatically altered the land. Over many millions of years, the rugged mountains eroded to the now familiar heavily wooded Appalachian Range that parallels the eastern coastline of North America. In Georgia the weathered metamorphic stone descended southeast toward the ancient Coastal Plain and the Atlantic Ocean, forming the foothills and river valleys of the present-day Piedmont Plateau. This process also exposed the domes of harder granite magma that we now know as Stone, Arabia, and Panola Mountains.

For thousands of years, the piedmont hills and valleys were notable for nearly unbroken forests of loblolly pines and deciduous trees, primarily red and white oaks, hickories, red maples, and flowering dogwoods. In earlier times, natives cleared small patches of forest for hunting and farming, but settlement, beginning in the 1830s, severely disturbed the land. In the Southern Piedmont, cotton farmers cleared huge areas of forest for agriculture that led to dramatic erosion and eventual abandonment. The Piedmont National Wildlife Refuge is an excellent example of forest restoration of such worn-out lands. To the north, small subsistence farms dominated on the nutrient-poor clay soils, and many settlers turned to logging to eke out a hardscrabble existence. Today, a hike in the piedmont woodlands around Atlanta reveals evidence of a century and a half of disturbance. In the increasingly urbanized environment, small pockets of woodland left relatively untouched may be highlighted by stands of mature hardwoods, while forests dominated by pines and grasses suggest a terrain that has been farmed or logged within the past century.

The hikes profiled in this book trace these diverse landscapes: the Southern Piedmont on peaks such as Kennesaw, Red Top, Pine, and Sawnee Mountains; along granite outcrops in the Stone, Arabia, and Panola Mountains; across river and stream valleys found along the Chattahoochee, Etowah, and Oconee Rivers, as well as Sweetwater, Little Mulberry, and Pine Log Creeks; and through the rolling, wooded hills at Laurel Ridge, Elachee, Charlie Elliott Wildlife Center, and Dauset Trails, each lush with pines, oaks, hickories, dogwoods, and a wide variety of native plants.

Two excellent sources for readers interested in learning more about the area's rich geological history are the award-winning *New Georgia Encyclopedia* (www.georgiaencyclopedia.org), and the popular guidebook *Roadside Geology of Georgia* (Mountainside Press, 2013).

Human History

The Atlanta area's human history may be traced back more than 10,000 years to when the first migrants, journeying south and east to escape the bitter conditions of the Ice Age, crossed the unbroken forests of the Piedmont Plateau in search of game. These early nomadic peoples traveled in small bands and left behind only faint traces of their passing.

Over many generations, bands grew larger and less nomadic, settling in small villages along major waterways such as the Etowah, Chattahoochee, and Ocmulgee Rivers. Natives of the Woodland Period (1000 BCE–800 CE) were well adapted to life in the piedmont forests and along the coast. Arrows replaced spears, allowing hunters to range farther in search of game, while agriculture advanced with abundant crops of corn and beans. The late Woodland and early Mississippian Periods (800–1540 CE) were marked by dramatic, and occasionally mysterious, ceremonial structures. Among these are the serpentine rock walls atop Fort Mountain, large ceremonial mounds erected on the Etowah River near Cartersville and above the Ocmulgee River north of Macon, and stacked stone cairns found at Little Mulberry Park near Auburn. The sixteenth-century arrival in Georgia of the first European explorers, Hernando De Soto and the Spanish conquistadores, led to inevitable clashes and decimation of the native people through war and disease.

Eventually the survivors coalesced into two nations, the Creek and the Cherokee. In 1821 leaders from both groups met near the home of Creek Chief William McIntosh (now the McIntosh Reserve) to set the Chattahoochee River as a rough boundary between the two peoples, with the Creek to the south and the Cherokee to the north. Four years later McIntosh, under enormous pressure from the government, signed the Treaty of Indian Springs, ceding nearly all Creek land in Georgia to the state. (He would be assassinated at his home a few months later by treaty opponents.) The Cherokee would also be forced out following the 1828 discovery of gold on their lands in northern Georgia near present-day Dahlonega. Within a decade, they were sent west to Oklahoma on the infamous "Trail of Tears." By the 1840s, nearly all the natives had been expelled from Georgia, opening lands in the fertile coastal plain and lower piedmont to large-scale, slavery-based cotton agriculture. The industrial and transportation centers of Augusta, Macon, and Columbus grew along the Fall Line, where cascading waters provided power for mills and factories.

The Cherokee removal opened northern Georgia for settlement, but it took the introduction of a new technology, the railroad, to spur the founding and growth of Atlanta. The city came into existence in 1837 as a construction camp called "Terminus" near the site where railroad surveyor Stephen H. Long drove a "zero mile post" marking the intersecting point of three railroads, the Western and Atlantic linking with Chattanooga, the Central of Georgia north from Savannah, and the Georgia Railroad expanding westward from Augusta.

Five years later, the rough-and-tumble village changed its name to "Marthasville," honoring the daughter of Governor Wilson Lumpkin, a strong railway advocate. On

Pumpkinvine Creek beside the trail, Pickett's Mill State Historic Site. See Hike 14.

Christmas Day 1842, the first train (hauled from Madison, Georgia, by oxen) departed from the depot for a 22-mile excursion to Marietta. In 1845 the growing town's civic leaders renamed it "Atlanta," a coined word foretelling its future as a link between the Atlantic Ocean and America's interior.

During the Civil War, Atlanta was the major transportation center for the Deep South and a strategic target for General William Tecumseh Sherman's invading Union Army. Fierce fighting took place in the spring and summer of 1864 as Yanks and Rebels battled at New Hope, Pickett's Mill, Kennesaw Mountain, and on the outskirts of the city. Historians believe that Atlanta's surrender and subsequent burning (chronicled in Margaret Mitchell's iconic *Gone with the Wind*) assured the reelection of Abraham Lincoln and the eventual defeat of the Confederacy.

In the quarter century following the war, Atlanta arose from the ashes to become what journalist Henry Grady dubbed a "brave and beautiful city." By the 1890s the city was the transportation and commercial center of the "New South." To celebrate its rebirth, Atlanta hosted the Cotton States International Exposition (the World's

Fair of its day) in a green space called Piedmont Park. Around the same time local businessman Asa Candler began marketing a new soft drink called Coca-Cola, which would take the world by storm and forever link Atlanta with the "pause that refreshes."

By the middle of the twentieth century, Atlanta began a period of unequalled and unabated growth. As the population expanded to a million and beyond, the small regional city was transformed into an international center of commerce and transportation. During the 1960s, the city found itself in the spotlight as home to the civil rights movement led by Atlanta-born Dr. Martin Luther King Jr. While other Southern cities succumbed to violence, Dr. King and local civic and business leaders worked tirelessly to present Atlanta as the city "too busy to hate" and as a model for nonviolent social change. A tangible outcome of these long-standing efforts was the selection of Atlanta to host the Centennial Olympic Games in 1996.

In recent years the city skyline has been transformed. Atlanta is home to several major corporations, and the railroads that brought Atlanta into existence were long ago overtaken by interstate highways and by countless flights from Hartsfield-Jackson Atlanta International Airport, the busiest in the world. With no shorelines or mountains to block its growth, Atlanta has sprawled in all directions, practically surrounding the neighboring cities of Marietta, Roswell, Decatur, Conyers, Jonesboro, and Douglasville.

This urbanization has focused increasing attention on the urgent need to preserve or reclaim vestiges of woodlands, waterways, and green spaces for outdoor recreation and enjoyment. Among these initiatives have been the establishment of the Chattahoochee River National Recreation Area along the city's northern boundaries (created during the presidency of Georgian Jimmy Carter); the development of networks of paved pathways and linear parks like the BeltLine, Silver Comet Trail, and the Big Creek and Suwanee Creek Greenways; the acquisition of lands for new parks such as Pine Mountain Recreation Area, Sawnee Mountain Preserve, and Little Mulberry Creek Park; and the setting aside of historic sites at Sweetwater Creek and Pickett's Mill Battlefield.

As Atlanta continues to grow and expand, parks and trails such as the ones profiled in this guide will become increasingly important resources for urban residents and visitors seeking to escape the city's hustle and bustle and reconnect with a natural world close to home.

Weather

Located more than 1,000 feet above sea level and in the heart of the Southern Piedmont, the Atlanta area is representative of a subtropical climate characterized by hot, humid summers and relatively mild winters. Historically, Atlanta has experienced approximately 50-plus inches of annual rainfall, but intermittent periods of drought have altered these figures in recent years.

Given the mild climate, Atlanta is blessed with good weather for hiking during every season of the year. Autumn is notable for the vivid colors of changing leaves,

Mountain laurel along the trail near Long Island Shoals. See Hike 1.

from the reds of the maples to the yellows of hickories and oranges of red and white oaks. Winter days are often chilly with only rare snow or ice, and a hike in the woods in this season reveals a more open landscape with the naked hardwood trees creating vistas invisible during other seasons. Spring in Atlanta is internationally renowned for the glorious cream-white colors of flowering dogwoods and multicolored hues of azalea blossoms blanketing the landscape. Summer offers vivid greens of hardwoods and pines in full foliage, with bright-colored wildflowers and rhododendron or mountain laurel blossoms punctuating the forest understory during May and June.

Rainfall tends to be fairly evenly distributed across the seasons. Autumn and winter rain is often more steady, of the all-day variety; while spring and summer are more prone to afternoon thunderstorms born from heat building up during the day. Rain patterns have been affected by the increasingly urban environment closer to downtown due to the creation of what atmospheric scientists describe as a "heat island," where a dome of more heated air created by automobile and industrial pollution raises temperatures inside the area three to four degrees above the surrounding countryside, another reason to escape the city for summertime hikes.

Weather Averages for Atlanta

Month	High	Low	Rainfall
January	52	34	4.20
February	57	38	4.67
March	65	44	4.81
April	73	52	3.36
May	80	60	3.67
June	86	68	3.95
July	89	71	5.27
August	88	71	3.90
September	82	65	4.47
October	73	54	3.41
November	64	45	4.10
December	54	37	3.90

(Weather Channel statistical averages, 1981–2010)

Tread Lightly on the Land

As noted in the previous section, the piedmont is a fragile landscape that may take a century or more to recover from damage. To preserve parks and trails for the enjoyment of all, please follow these recommendations:

- Follow all posted park or trail use rules. Avoid taking shortcuts as this may accelerate erosion.
- If pets are permitted on the trails, please keep them leashed so they do not disturb other trail users or local wildlife. Carry bags to remove any solid pet waste.
- Follow trail etiquette. Bicyclists yield to equestrians, runners, and hikers, and keep your bike under control and at a safe speed. Runners and hikers yield to equestrians. Downhill traffic should yield to uphill traffic. Warn people when you are planning to pass. Use your voice to warn equestrians, not bells or horns, as these

may frighten horses. When a horse approaches, move off the trail. (Source: Trail Etiquette 101 from Leave No Trace Center for Outdoor Ethics; www.lnt.org)

- Leave the areas as you found them (or better) by packing out your trash and disposing of it properly.

- Enjoy observing wildlife from a respectful distance. You may wish to pack a camera, binoculars, or sketchbook to record your observations.

- Treat hikes with children as both an adventure and an opportunity to instill in them an appreciation for the environment. Pack a nature guide to help them learn about the features and creatures in the world around them. When planning a trek with children, consider the difficulty in distance and terrain so that it matches their interests and stamina. Encourage children with extra snacks to keep up their energy levels and remember to pack tissue for their personal hygiene.

- The familiar phrase "take nothing but pictures and leave nothing but footprints" sums up what it means to tread lightly on the land.

Enjoying the Hike

While the trails listed in this guide are easily accessible and of moderate distance, some preparation is important to fully enjoy the trek.

Getting in shape. Good physical conditioning and stamina are essential for enjoying a hike of more than a few miles. Prepare with regular walking of comparable distances. Before you tackle the summits of Kennesaw, Sawnee, or Stone Mountains, begin by taking the stairs more often, or finding hills in your neighborhood to climb. You may also wish to join a gym where you might supplement your conditioning program with work on treadmills and stair-climbing equipment. When planning a group outing, consider the condition and stamina of the weakest member when choosing your destination.

Basic first aid. "Be Prepared" is more than the Boy Scouts' motto. It is solid advice when planning a hike in the woods, where you may be a few miles from a car or from assistance if an accident happens. While nearly all of the hikes profiled in the book are close to population centers, it is a good idea to pack a few basic first-aid items in your pack. Some supplies to consider include insect repellent, cleansing wipes, adhesive bandages, antibiotic ointment for cuts and scrapes, an elastic wrap for sprains and strains, moleskin to cover blisters, antihistamine tablets for allergic reactions to insect bites or stings, tweezers to remove splinters, sunscreen (SPF 15 or higher), and aspirin or acetaminophen for pain. Many of these essential items are neatly packed in small first-aid kits available from outdoor equipment stores.

Planning Your Hike

Nearly all of the trails profiled in this guide are within about an hour's drive from the city. When choosing a hiking destination, consider the trail location, times of traffic

Midtown skyline from Oak Hill in Piedmont Park. See Hike 20.

congestion, hike distance and difficulty, weather, and personal interests. In every case, a little advance planning will make your hike more enjoyable.

Clothing. Moderate weather in the Atlanta area and surrounding piedmont allows for enjoyable hiking at any time of year, provided you dress accordingly. Hot and humid summer days call for breathable fabrics that wick moisture away from your body, a hat, and sunscreen; layering warm clothing and outerwear can take the chill out of a winter hike. Weather may change quickly, especially in summer when surface heating might spawn pop-up thunderstorms, so it is always a good idea to stuff a windbreaker or rain jacket in your pack. When hiking with children, they often need to be reminded to add a layer as their bodies are affected by the weather more quickly than adults, so be certain that they have the proper clothing for the trek.

Footwear. While heavy-duty hiking boots are certainly suitable for the moderate-distance hikes profiled in the guide, you may be just as happy with lightweight, all-terrain walking shoes with solid, lug-type soles. There are a wide variety of styles and brands from which to choose, so you may wish to visit a local outdoor equipment retailer to find a pair that fit both your feet and your budget. Also, don't forget to include a pair of good-quality hiking socks to go along with your shoes.

Food and water. For even a short hike, it is a good idea to pack high-energy snacks and extra water. On the hottest summer or coldest winter days, hydration and a quick energy boost may be just what are needed to assure an enjoyable trek. If you are hiking with children or pets, consider their needs as well when packing supplies for the hike.

Personal safety. While the overwhelming majority of other trail users are also seeking outdoor recreation and enjoyment, in the Atlanta area's increasingly urban environment, it is always wise to be alert to your personal safety on the trail.

Be alert to your surroundings; carry a whistle and/or pepper spray and a cell phone. If you observe people acting suspiciously or feel threatened, do not hesitate to leave the area and use a cell phone to call 911 for assistance. Most of the profiled hiking trails are within cell phone coverage areas.

Let family and friends know your plans. Provide information on where you are going and when you expect to return.

Hiking with a companion or group provides the safety of numbers. This is a great way to share your experience and learn from others. There are a number of outdoor clubs in the Atlanta area, and you will find a selection of them in Appendix B.

While you are unlikely to encounter snakes, it is important to be aware that piedmont woodlands and wetlands are native habitat for three species of venomous snakes: copperheads (most common), pigmy and timber rattlesnakes, and cottonmouths (Southern Piedmont).

Piedmont forests are also habitat for black-legged or deer ticks that carry Lyme disease. It is advisable when hiking through grassy areas, especially in summer, to wear long pants or hiking socks, use insect repellent, and to inspect for ticks when bathing after a hike. Parents should be diligent in checking children for ticks after an outing. With proper precautions both before and after a hike, the risks of tick-borne illness may be greatly minimized.

Using Map, Compass, and Global Positioning System (GPS) Devices

All of the trails described in this guide are well maintained, and most are marked or blazed. Following the included map will keep you on the right path, or you may choose a more detailed topographical map available from an outdoor equipment retailer, from various software programs such as DeLorme TOPO North America, or online from the US Geological Survey (www.usgs.gov), Gaia GPS (www.gaiagps.com), Map My Walk (www.mapmywalk.com), and other applications for computers, tablets, and smartphones. You may also wish to carry a compass or GPS device to enhance your skills with these navigation tools. Using all three in combination is an excellent way to check your current location and your direction of travel, as well as the terrain around you and ahead. You may also be interested in improving your skills by joining affinity groups that turn navigation into adventures. Check these out:

Orienteering is the sport of navigating a course from start to finish by following map and compass directions to predetermined way points. It can be enjoyed as a leisure activity or in event competitions. To learn more, contact the Georgia Orienteering Club at www.gaorienteering.org.

Geocaching is a scavenger hunt gone high-tech. Individuals or groups have hidden caches (usually a small waterproof container with a logbook and some small rewards) in parks and public places around the world. They share the GPS coordinates for the cache and invite others to find them. Once found, the individual is usually asked to sign the log, take a reward, and to leave something in the box for the next searcher. Geocaching is a great way to improve skills with GPS devices, and many of the parks and trails listed in this guide contain geocaches. To learn more visit www .geocaching.com.

Getting to the Trail

Nearly all the trails in the guide are convenient to one of the three interstate highways that intersect in downtown Atlanta (I-75, I-85, and I-20) or other major highways, and each chapter provides detailed directions from highways to the trailhead. A street-level map or atlas (available from retailers, printed from a software program like DeLorme Street Atlas or Topo North America, or downloaded from an Internet source such as Google Maps or Waze) will supplement the printed directions or help you find alternatives in the event of a traffic delay. With Atlanta's traffic congestion, you may wish to select your hikes based on day of the week, the time you have available, traffic conditions, and travel distance to the trailhead.

Using This Guide

Best Hikes Atlanta is divided into four sections: National Park Service Units, U.S. Army Corps of Engineers, Georgia Department of Natural Resources, and Local Parks and Gardens. When possible, within each section entries are listed in a clockwise direction beginning in the northwest. Entries include all the essential information to find and enjoy a hike suited to your time, interests, and physical condition.

Trails are rated on degrees of difficulty from easy to strenuous. These ratings are more a measure of elevation gain or loss over distance and trail surface than the length of the trail. A 5-mile hike over the summit of Kennesaw Mountain may be listed as strenuous while a trek of greater distance, such as a 6-mile walk on the mostly level Big Creek Greenway, may be listed as easy. The ratings should be used only as a general guide.

All of the listed trails are well maintained, and many are identified with color-coded or other types of trail blazes or markings. You should follow maps closely and refer to written hike descriptions to confirm your course and direction, especially when approaching intersections.

The trail maps provide all the information you need to enjoy the hike, including basic topographical changes, key landmarks, and intersections. In addition, several trails offer online maps that may be downloaded to a tablet or smartphone, or printed to supplement those contained in the guide. While a compass or GPS device is not necessary on any of these marked trails, they may enhance your enjoyment of the trek. For this reason, we include a selection of GPS coordinates with each trail description as another tool for finding your way.

A number of these trails serve multiple users. In each trail description we note if the park is open to other users, most notably equestrians, bicyclists, and inline skaters. It is important to follow trail etiquette when sharing the path with others.

Some of the listed trails are suitable for mobility-impaired travelers utilizing wheelchairs and motorized scooters. Especially suitable for these visitors are the paved pathways in Piedmont Park and the BeltLine, along the Silver Comet, Big Creek, and Suwanee Creek Greenways; the Cochran Shoals Fitness Trail in the Chattahoochee River National Recreation Area; ADA-accessible paths at Red Top Mountain State Park; sidewalks at Stone Mountain Park; and portions of the trail system at Little Mulberry Park.

Enjoy and Respect This Beautiful Landscape

As you take advantage of the spectacular scenery offered by the Atlanta area, remember that our planet is very dear, very special, and very fragile. All of us should do everything we can to keep it clean, beautiful, and healthy, including following the Green Tips you'll find throughout this book.

Remember, the *best hike* is only footsteps away!

Map Legend

Roads

75	Freeway/Interstate Highway
41	US Highway
401	State Highway
	Other Road
	Unpaved Road
	Railroad

Trails

	Selected Route
	Trail or Fire Road
	Paved Trail or Bike Path
	Boardwalk/Steps
	Direction of Travel

Water Features

	Body of Water
	River or Creek
	Marsh or Wetland
	Waterfall

Land Management

	Parks and Preserves

Map Symbols

20	Trailhead
	Picnic Area
?	Visitor Center/Information
P	Parking
	Restroom
	Water
	Lodging
	Restaurant
	Campground
	Ranger Station
	Handicapped Access
	Boat Launch
	Gate
	Bridge
	Mountain/Peak
	Building/Point of Interest
	Scenic View
	Major Airport
N	True North (Magnetic North is approximately 15.5° East)

Trail Finder

Tips for finding the perfect trail to suit your interest.

Hike No.	Hike Name	Best Hikes with Children	Best Hikes for Great Mountain Views	Best Hikes for Nature Lovers
1	West Palisades Unit Trails			•
2	East Palisades Unit Trails			•
3	Cochran Shoals Unit Trails	•		•
4	Sope Creek Unit Trails			•
5	Gold Branch Unit Trails			•
6	Vickery Creek Unit Trails			•
7	Island Ford Unit Trails			•
8	Jones Bridge Unit Trails			•
9	Summit to Pigeon Hill Trails Loop			•
10	Cheatham Hill to Pigeon Hill Trails Loop			•
11	Cheatham Hill to Kolb Farm Trails Loop			•
12	Piedmont National Wildlife Refuge Trails			•
13	Laurel Ridge Trail on Lake Sidney Lanier			
14	Pickett's Mill State Historic Site Trails Historic Site Trails	•		
15	Red Top Mountain State Park: Homestead and Sweetgum Trails			
16	Red Top Mountain State Park: Iron Hill Multiuse Trail			•
17	Amicalola Falls State Park Trails		•	•
18	Sweetwater Creek State Conservation Park Trails			•
19	Charlie Elliott Wildlife Center			•
20	Piedmont Park Trails	•		

Best Hikes for Lake Lovers	Best Hikes for Waterfalls	Best Hikes for Geology Lovers	Best Hikes for History Buffs	Best Hikes for People Watching	Best Hikes for Dogs	Best Hikes to Bring Your Mountain Bike
				•	•	•
	•					
		•	•			
		•	•			
		•	•			
•						
			•			
•						
•						•
	•					
		•	•			
			•	•	•	

Hike No.	Hike Name	Best Hikes with Children	Best Hikes for Great Mountain Views	Best Hikes for Nature Lovers
21	BeltLine Eastside Trail	•		
22	Silver Comet Trail: Mavell Road to Floyd Road			
23	Silver Comet Trail: Floyd Road to Florence Road			
24	Pine Mountain Recreation Area Trails		•	
25	Pine Log Creek Trails			•
26	Big Creek Greenway Trail	•		
27	Suwanee Creek Greenway Trail	•		
28	Sawnee Mountain Preserve: Indian Seats Trails		•	
29	Sawnee Mountain Preserve: Mountainside Trails	•		•
30	Elachee Nature Science Center at Chicopee Woods Nature Preserve	•		•
31	Little Mulberry Park Trails	•		
32	State Botanical Garden of Georgia	•		•
33	Stone Mountain Park: Cherokee Trail and Upper Walk-Up Trail		•	
34	Davidson-Arabia Mountain Nature Preserve	•	•	
35	Dauset Trails Nature Center	•		
36	Cochran Mill Park	•		
37	McIntosh Reserve			•

Best Hikes for Lake Lovers	Best Hikes for Waterfalls	Best Hikes for Geology Lovers	Best Hikes for History Buffs	Best Hikes for People Watching	Best Hikes for Dogs	Best Hikes to Bring Your Mountain Bike
			●	●		
				●		●
						●
		●				●
		●				
					●	●
					●	●
		●		●		
		●				
		●			●	
		●				
						●
	●					
			●			

National Park Service Units

Chattahoochee River National Recreation Area

Established in 1978 during the presidency of Georgian Jimmy Carter, the Chattahoochee River National Recreation area protects nearly 11,000 acres in 16 units along 48 miles of the river. The units feature more than 60 miles of foot and biking trails that draw nearly three million visitors annually to hike, bike, fish, and boat only a short distance from Atlanta. Most park trails are marked with blue blazes and feature "you are here" informational tablets at major intersections.

GREEN TIP
Carpool or take public transportation to the trailhead.

◀ *Trail near Devil's Race Course Shoals. See Hike 1.*

1 West Palisades Unit Trails

Located along I-75, West Palisades preserves a scenic and historic landscape. Pioneers John and Hardy Pace settled here shortly after the land was ceded by the Creeks, and Hardy operated a mill and ferry near the current site of Pace's Ferry Road in nearby Vinings. For many years, Pace's Mill and another mill operated by the Akers family served as gathering places for local farmers. Today only the road names survive as evidence of these long-vanished community landmarks. West Palisades features riverside and upland trails, sheer stone outcrops, and river shoals offering excellent fly-fishing and birding.

Start: Large parking area adjacent to comfort station and recreation field
Distance: 5.5-mile lollipop with a linear access trail to a circuit of interconnected loops
Approximate hiking time: 3 hours
Elevation gain/loss: 215 feet
Trail surface: Compacted soil and gravel
Lay of the land: River floodplain and upland mixed forest
Difficulty: Moderate to strenuous due to distance and steep, occasionally rocky, terrain
Seasons: Trails are especially beautiful in spring and autumn

Canine compatibility: Leashed dogs permitted
Land status: National Park Service
Fees and permits: Daily pass; annual pass available for all units
Schedule: Open dawn to dark
Nearest town: Vinings
Maps: USGS Sandy Springs; maps also available from park website (maps are downloadable to tablet or smartphone with QR code and marked waypoints)
Trail contact: Chattahoochee River National Recreation Area, 1978 Island Ford Rd., Atlanta 30350; (678) 538-1200; www.nps.gov/chat

Finding the trailhead: From Atlanta, travel north on I-75 to Mount Paran Road (exit 266). Turn left (west), then immediately turn right (north) on US 41. After crossing the Chattahoochee River, turn right at the Chattahoochee River National Recreation Area sign and follow the access road to the parking area. There is also a satellite parking area off Akers Ridge Drive. GPS: N33 52.244' / W84 27.187'

The Hike

From the parking area, you will travel north past a comfort station and recreation field. The trail bends around the field and enters a wide, graveled, heavily shaded corridor that follows the banks of the Chattahoochee River. At 0.8 mile, the path passes beneath the busy I-75 bridge. A short distance ahead is a rest area and beyond that a wooden footbridge across Rottenwood Creek.

On the far side of the bridge, reach a T intersection. The paved path to the left is part of the Bob Callan Trail system, linking an increasing number of destinations in the Cumberland Mall area. Turn right and follow the river trail, now narrowed and composed of compacted soil, as it winds along the water, offering vistas of rocky

Along the gravel trail

shoals and small cascades. Cross a rock outcrop and at 1.4 miles, the path reaches a forked intersection. Turn left (the trail to the right leads 0.2 mile to rocky cliffs that are hazardous to climb), and begin a steady ascent away from the river. Following a climb of 0.4 mile, the trail intersects with the trail ascending from Rottenwood Creek. Turn right and continue ascending steeply to a wooded ridge crest. The path then follows a level course along the ridge and through an upland forest of pines, oaks, and hickories for about a half mile before descending again to a trail intersection at 2.2 miles (the path straight from this intersection exits the park behind an apartment complex on Chattahoochee Summit Drive).

Turn right and continue descending along a switchback, crossing an intermittent stream, before climbing to an intersection at 2.6 miles. The path to the left leads 0.3 mile to a satellite parking area on Akers Ridge Drive (reached from Akers Mill Road and Akers Drive). Bear right and begin a steady descent to the river floodplain on an old, broken pavement and gravel road.

Reach a trail marker at 2.7 miles and continue straight, past a meadow, before reaching the site of an old boat ramp. Bear to the left, past the ramp, and hike north past a new boat ramp and seasonal comfort station as the trail follows the water to Devil's Race Course Shoals and the park's northern boundary. From the shoals, return past the ramp, and continue along the riverbank. The path will trace a loop, crossing a footbridge then bending right on a return to the previous trail marker. Retrace your steps up the old road to the intersection and turn left again to return to

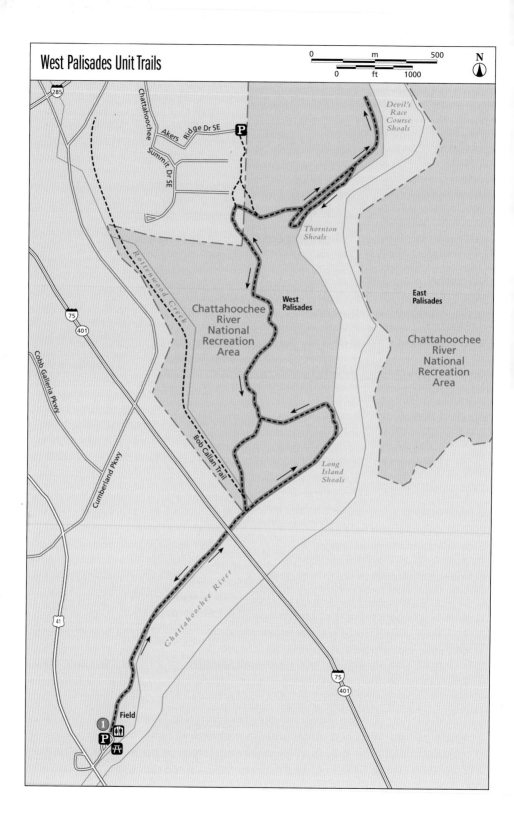

West Palisades Unit Trails

0 — m — 500
0 — ft — 1000

N

285

Chattahoochee

Akers Ridge Dr SE

P

Summit Dr SE

Devil's
Race
Course
Shoals

Rollenwood Creek

75

401

Thornton
Shoals

West
Palisades

East
Palisades

Chattahoochee
River
National
Recreation
Area

Chattahoochee
River
National
Recreation
Area

Cobb Galleria Pkwy

Cumberland Pkwy

Bob Callan Trail

Long
Island
Shoals

41

Chattahoochee River

75
401

Field

1

P

Chattahoochee River from trail

the main trail. Turn left and follow the path over the ridge crest and descend to the bridge at Rottenwood Creek. Re-cross the footbridge and pass beneath I-75, returning on the gravel path to the starting point at 5.5 miles.

Miles and Directions

0.0 Start the hike by the recreation field. GPS: N33 52.244' / W84 27.187'

0.8 Reach the bridge over Rottenwood Creek. GPS: N33 52.611' / W84 26.895'

1.4 At the trail intersection, turn left and ascend away from river. GPS: N33 52.873' / W84 26.691'

1.8 At the intersection the trail ascends from Rottenwood Creek. GPS: N33 52.858' / W84 26.844'

2.6 Turn right at the intersection for the trail to Devil's Race Course Shoals. GPS: N33 53.172' / W84 26.914'

3.1 You have reached Devil's Race Course Shoals. GPS: N33 53.386' / W84 26.566'

5.5 The return loop brings you back to the starting point.

GREEN TIP
If you're toting food, leave the packaging at home. Repack your provisions in ziplock bags that you can reuse and that can double as garbage bags on the way out of the woods.

2 East Palisades Unit Trails

This unit of the Chattahoochee River offers a taste of rugged beauty from high, heavily wooded ridges above the water to sandy, lushly carpeted floodplains lined with ferns and willows. Late autumn and winter are ideal seasons for hiking here as the leafless trees offer panoramic vistas of the river and surrounding hills.

Start: Gravel parking area off Indian Trail Road
Distance: 4.3-mile loop of interconnecting trails
Approximate hiking time: 2 to 3 hours
Elevation gain/loss: 231 feet
Trail surface: Compact dirt, sandy floodplain
Lay of the land: Wooded ridges and slopes, river floodplain
Difficulty: Moderate to strenuous due to distance and steep terrain
Seasons: Year-round
Canine compatibility: Leashed dogs permitted
Land status: National Park Service

Fees and permits: Daily pass; annual pass available (all units)
Schedule: Open daily dawn to dark
Nearest town: Sandy Springs
Maps: USGS Sandy Springs; maps also available from the park website (maps are downloadable to tablet or smartphone with QR code and marked waypoints)
Trail contact: Chattahoochee River National Recreation Area, 1978 Island Ford Parkway, Atlanta 30350; (678) 538-1200; www.nps .gov/chat

Finding the trailhead: From I-285, follow Riverside Drive (exit 24) south for 0.5 mile to Mount Vernon Road. Bear right (west) and travel 1.2 miles, where Mount Vernon merges with Northside Drive. Follow Northside Drive for 0.5 mile and turn right (west) on Indian Trail Road. Continue on Indian Trail, past the park entrance where the road becomes gravel. Drive about a mile to the parking area. (*Note:* The road is narrow so be alert to oncoming vehicles.) GPS: N33 53.061' / W84 26.196'

The Hike

From the parking area, the trail enters the woods beside an information board, steadily descending to the southwest toward the river floodplain. A short distance ahead, note the fading ruins of buildings to the right of the trail, evidence of long vanished homes slowly being reclaimed by nature. Along this section, portions of the path are moderately eroded, and log steps have been installed to slow further deterioration. The trail reaches a lush bottomland area above the banks by Long Island Creek before crossing a stream by a footbridge at 0.4 mile. A second bridge leads across the creek to a satellite parking area off Whitewater Creek Drive.

The path bends sharply northward and follows the Chattahoochee River floodplain, past stands of river cane, before crossing a small bridge over Charlie's Trapping

Trail along the Chattahoochee River bank ▶

On trail looking back at Interstate 75 bridge

Creek at 1.0 mile. At a nearby marked intersection, bear left and continue to follow the river. At 1.3 miles, an unblazed path continues straight while the main, blue-blazed trail bends right and begins to climb steadily away from the water. Turn right at the next marked intersection (the side trail to the left leads 0.1 mile down to Thornton Shoals) and continue to ascend more steeply on switchbacks as the path follows the slope upward, reaching a ridge high above the water at 1.8 miles.

Follow the path along the ridgeline and through an upland mixed forest, bearing left at a signed intersection. A short distance ahead, turn left again at another marked intersection. The trail quickly and steeply descends on log steps to a wooden overlook platform with a panoramic view to the northwest. The vista includes Devil's Race Course Shoals, the West Palisades Unit of the park on the opposite bank, and buildings along I-285 in the distance.

As you exit the platform, turn left on a narrow path as it bends right to an intersection with the main trail. At this point, you may choose to turn sharply left and descend, at times steeply, on a linear trail along a heavily wooded slope and across a boardwalk that leads to the floodplain at Devil's Race Course Shoals. The round-trip on this side trail will add 1.5 miles to your hike.

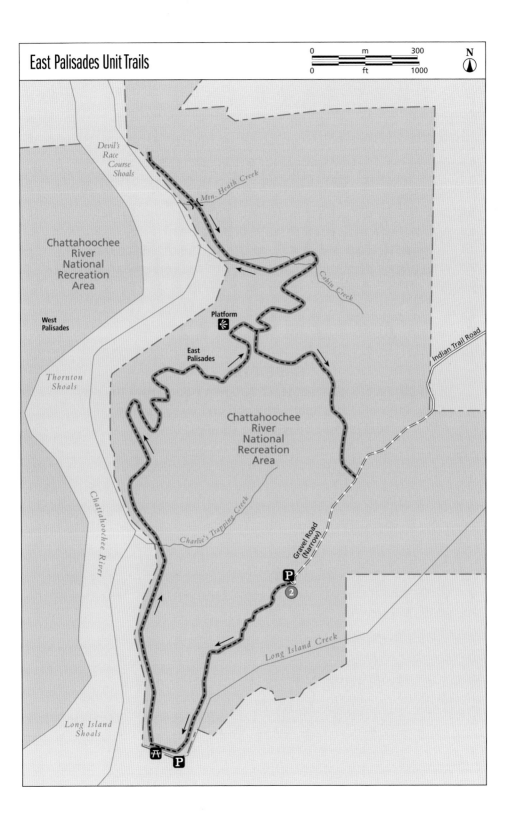

East Palisades Unit Trails

0   m   300
0   ft   1000

N

Devil's
Race
Course
Shoals

Mtn. Heath Creek

Cabin Creek

Chattahoochee
River
National
Recreation
Area

West
Palisades

Thornton
Shoals

Platform

East
Palisades

Indian Trail Road

Chattahoochee
River
National
Recreation
Area

Chattahoochee River

Charlie's Trapping Creek

Gravel Road
(Narrow)

P

2

Long Island Creek

Long Island
Shoals

P

Retrace your steps from the intersection with the Devil's Race Course Shoals access trail. Follow the main trail along the upper slopes of the ridge, bending left and climbing back to the gravel access road. Turn right and follow the road for 0.3 mile, returning to the parking area at 4.3 miles (including the hike down to the shoals).

Miles and Directions

0.0   Begin the hike at the gravel parking area. GPS: N33 53.061' / W84 26.196'

0.6   Reach a bridge near a satellite parking area at Whitewater Creek Drive. GPS: N33 52.706' / W84 26.524'

1.0   Cross the bridge over Charlie's Trapping Creek. GPS: N33 53.036' / W84 26.541'

1.8   Reach the crest of the ridge. GPS: N33 53.286' / W84 26.513'

2.1   The platform provides an overlook of the river. GPS: N33 53.382' / W84 26.376'

2.9   At this point you have reached the end of the one-way trail to the river floodplain by Devil's Race Course Shoals. Retrace your steps to return to the main trail. GPS: N33 53.590' / W84 26.523'

4.0   When you reach the gravel entrance road, turn right.

4.3   After the short return on the gravel road, reach the starting point.

GREEN TIP
Wash dishes or clothes at least 200 feet from a river or lake. Bring the water to a spot with good drainage, and use only biodegradable soap in the smallest amount.

3 Cochran Shoals Unit Trails

With its 3.1-mile gravel Fitness Trail, the Cochran Shoals Unit, located just off I-285, is the national recreation area's busiest (the parking area can quickly fill to capacity on weekends). Beyond the Fitness Trail are challenging hiking and mountain-biking paths that climb into the surrounding hills, including the Scribner Trail linking Cochran Shoals with the Sope Creek Unit of the park.

Start: Cochran Shoals parking area (Columns Drive or Powers Island are alternates)
Distance: 6.1 miles of interconnected loops
Approximate hiking time: 3 to 4 hours
Elevation gain/loss: 170 feet
Trail surface: Fine gravel, wooden boardwalks, compact dirt, and sandy floodplain
Lay of the land: River floodplain and upland slopes
Difficulty: Moderate
Seasons: Year-round
Other trail users: Bicyclists
Canine compatibility: Leashed dogs permitted

Land status: National Park Service
Fees and permits: Daily pass; annual pass available (all units)
Nearest town: Sandy Springs
Maps: USGS Sandy Springs; maps also available from the park website (maps are downloadable to tablet or smartphone with QR code and marked waypoints)
Trail contact: Chattahoochee River National Recreation Area, 1978 Island Ford Parkway, Atlanta 30350; (678) 538-1200; www.nps .gov/chat

Finding the trailhead: From I-285, exit on Northside Drive/New Northside Drive (exit 22). From the exit, drive north on I-Parkway North. The parkway curves to the left (west) and descends first to the Powers Island parking area, then across the river to the Cochran Shoals parking area. The entrances to the two units are about 0.3 mile apart. GPS: N33 54.113' / W84 26.411'

There is a satellite parking area on Columns Drive at the north end of the Cochran Shoals Unit. It may be reached by exiting I-285 at Riverside Drive (exit 24) and traveling north for 2.4 miles to Johnson Ferry Road. Turn left (north), crossing the Chattahoochee River past the CRNRA Johnson Ferry Unit, and turn left (south) on Columns Drive at 1.0 mile. The road winds through the Johnson Ferry Unit before reaching a parking area for Cochran Shoals at 2.6 miles. GPS: N33 55.306' / W 84 26.342'

The Hike

Beginning from the Cochran Shoals parking lot, pass the information board and walk along the wide, gravel Fitness Trail that follows the river. At 0.5 mile, bear left and follow the Gunby Trail over a boardwalk, then through a lowland marsh area. You will reach a signed intersection; continue straight on a narrow footpath that ascends to a power-line corridor. Cross the open area and continue along the Gunby Trail as it climbs toward the park boundary by an office building at 1.3 miles.

Boardwalk to Gunby Trail from Fitness Trail

The trail bends right and ascends a short distance before turning right again as it closes the loop. After a short distance the path reaches a ridgeline before beginning a gentle descent to a signed intersection. Turn left and descend along the slope toward a bottomland creek bed. Cross a footbridge over an intermittent stream at 1.8 miles and bend right; cross a second bridge as the path winds through a lowland area before rejoining the Fitness Trail at 2.4 miles.

Turn left and cross a footbridge, passing two short side trails. The trail to the left leads into the surrounding hills while the path to the right leads to a return to the parking area. Pass the intersection with the Scribner Trail that connects with the Sope Creek Unit and continue straight. Turn left at 3.0 miles on the multiuse trail (be alert for bicyclists) and ascend past the intersection of the bike trail. The path follows the slope on a winding course before reaching a sharp right turn at 4.1 miles and descending back to a left turn on the Fitness Trail. Bend right at the Columns Drive entrance and continue following the Fitness Trail on the return loop toward the starting point.

At 5.0 miles, pass a short path to a river observation deck before crossing a footbridge. Continue on the Fitness Trail, returning to the parking area at 6.1 miles.

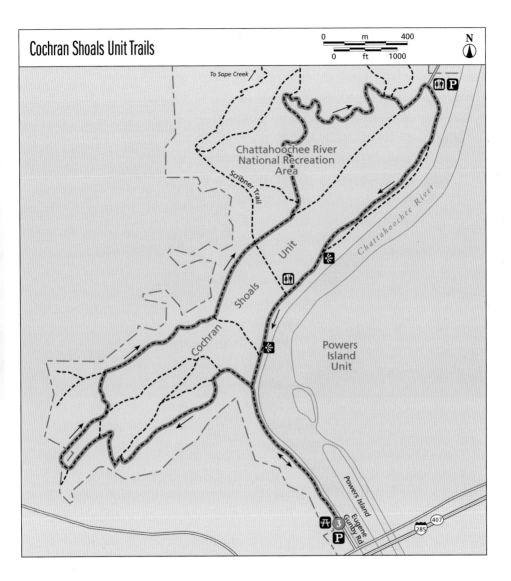

To Sope Creek

Chattahoochee River
National Recreation
Area

Scribner Trail

Unit

Shoals

Cochran

Chattahoochee River

Powers
Island
Unit

Powers Island

Eugene
Gunby Rd

285

407

Miles and Directions

0.0 Begin the hike at the Cochran Shoals parking area with information kiosk and picnic tables. GPS: N33 54.113' / W84 26.411'

0.5 At the intersection of Gunby Trail on the left, follow the Gunby Trail across the boardwalk into marsh and woodland area. GPS: N33 54.320' / W84 26.562'

0.7 After crossing the boardwalk, go straight following the narrow, dirt path.

1.3 The trail bends right at the park boundary by a large office building. From here you will begin your return loop. GPS: N33 54.339' / W84 27.528'

1.8 Cross a footbridge over a stream and turn right.

Cochran Shoals Multiuse Trail

2.4 Descend out of the woods to rejoin the Cochran Shoals Fitness Trail and turn left. GPS: N33 54.473' / W84 27.387'

2.8 The intersection of the Scribner Trail is on the left, but you will continue straight.

3.0 Bear left at the signpost on the multiuse trail and ascend. Be alert to bicyclists on this section of trail. GPS: N33 54.980' / W84 26.729'

3.5 Bear right and descend on multiuse trail.

4.1 Turn right from multiuse trail at the signpost and descend a short distance to the Fitness Trail. Turn left.

4.2 When you reach the Columns Drive entrance, turn right on the inner loop. GPS: N33 55.268' / W84 26.390'

5.0 On the left is an observation deck with a view of the river. GPS: N33 54.747' / W84 26.814'

6.1 After passing the intersection of the Gunby Trail, return to the Cochran Shoals parking area.

GREEN TIP

Avoid sensitive ecological areas. Hike, rest, and camp at least 200 feet from streams, lakes, and rivers.

4 Sope Creek Unit Trails

This park unit preserves woodlands and river bottomlands surrounding the site of the nineteenth-century Marietta Paper Mill on the banks of Sope Creek. While the origins of the creek's name are obscure, it is believed to come from Cherokee Chief "Sope," who lived in the area in the early 1800s. The original mill was constructed by slaves in the 1850s; it produced paper for Confederate currency during the Civil War. The mill, spared by Union forces in 1864, succumbed to fire in the 1870s. The rebuilt mill closed in 1903, and the abandoned buildings slowly deteriorated to the ruins seen today.

Start: Parking area off Paper Mill Road

Distance: 5.3-mile circuit hike of interconnected loops

Approximate hiking time: 3 hours

Elevation gain/loss: 156 feet

Trail surface: Compacted soil

Lay of the land: Wooded slopes, bottomlands

Difficulty: Moderate to strenuous due to distance and steep terrain

Seasons: Year-round

Canine compatibility: Leashed dogs permitted

Land status: National Park Service

Fees and permits: Daily pass; annual pass available (all units)

Schedule: Open dawn to dark

Nearest town: Sandy Springs

Maps: USGS Sandy Springs; maps also available at park website (maps are downloadable to tablet or smartphone with QR code and marked waypoints)

Trail contact: Chattahoochee River National Recreation Area, 1978 Island Ford Parkway, Atlanta 30350; (678) 538-1200; www.nps .gov/chat

Finding the trailhead: Travel north on GA 400 to Abernathy Road (exit 5) toward Sandy Springs. Turn right (west) at the end of the ramp. Follow Abernathy for 2.1 miles, crossing Roswell Road, before bending right (north) on Johnson Ferry Road. Descend to the bridge across the Chattahoochee River, past the Johnson Ferry Road Unit of the national recreation area. After 1.5 miles turn left (west) on Paper Mill Road. Follow Paper Mill for 2.1 miles, turning sharply right (west) across the bridge over Sope Creek. In a short distance, turn left (south) at the park entrance sign. The trail begins at the far end of the parking area. GPS: N33 56.282' / W84 26.597'

The Hike

The marked trail begins at the end of the paved parking area, descending along the mixed-use Fox Creek Trail (hiking/mountain biking). At 0.1 mile, bear right above Sibley Pond and follow the path along the bank. At the far end of the pond, a side trail to the right traces a half-mile loop along heavily wooded slopes, across intermittent creek beds, and through a meadow before reconnecting with the main trail. Bear right and follow a level path that soon merges with the Fox Creek Trail at 0.8 mile.

After a series of climbs and descents, sometimes over exposed rocks, the trail reaches Fox Creek at 1.5 miles. The Fox Creek Trail continues straight as it connects

Autumn leaves on Sope Creek Trail

with the Cochran Shoals Unit of the Chattahoochee River National Recreation Area. Turn left and follow the north bank of the creek. In about a half mile, pass an apartment complex and cross a footbridge, ascending past a trail intersection on the left. Continue straight as the trail bends north and follows the slope above Sope Creek. At 2.6 miles, bend sharply right and begin a steady descent toward a streambed.

Cross the stream and ascend the slope before bending west and then sharply right on a switchback. At the trail intersection turn left, then bear right and climb across a series of ridges on a northeastward route. At the trail intersection, continue straight

PATH TO VICTORY

On July 5, 1864, Union cavalry troopers, under command of Gen. Kenner Garrard, were scouting for a place to ford the Chattahoochee and discovered an old fish dam across the river below Sope Creek. Only a handful of Rebel soldiers were seen guarding the ford and were unaware of the reconnaissance. The men reported their discovery to Garrard, and two days later, federal troops crossed the river at this point, forcing the Confederates to withdraw all of their forces south of the Chattahoochee to the outer defenses of Atlanta.

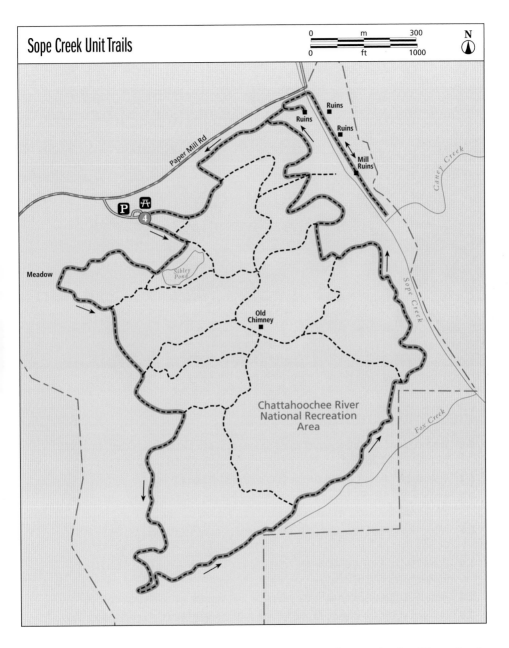

Sope Creek Unit Trails

and descend to the right to reach the mill ruins above the west bank of Sope Creek. At 4.0 miles, cross the bridge over the creek and turn right to follow the linear trail past additional ruins of the nineteenth-century paper mill.

To return to the parking area, retrace your steps across the bridge and follow the path a short distance, bending left and ascending back into the woods. Turn right at the intersection and follow the path back to the starting point at 5.3 miles.

Old mill ruins on Sope Creek

Miles and Directions

0.0 The trail begins at eastern end of paved parking area with picnic tables nearby. GPS: N33 56.282' / W84 26.597'

0.1 Bear right on the foot trail that follows the north end of Sibley Pond.

0.2 Take the side trail that traces a loop along heavily wooded slopes, through intermittent creek beds, and across a meadow.

0.8 When the side trail reconnects with the main trail, turn right. GPS: N33 56.099' / W84 26.563'

1.8 Leave Fox Creek Trail just above the creek and turn left along hiking path. GPS: N33 55.692' / W84 26.579'

2.3 Pass an apartment complex on the left as the trail ascends across a footbridge.

2.6 Descend across the streambed and follow a switchbacking ascent of several ridges and past connecting trails.

4.0 At the trail intersection, turn right to descend to the ruins of the paper mill and Sope Creek Bridge. GPS: N33 56.434' / W84 26.252'

4.4 Cross the bridge to follow the path to the mill ruins on the eastern side of the creek. GPS: N33 56.315' / W84 26.135'

4.7 Ascend into the woods south of Paper Mill Road and continue on this trail back to starting point.

5.3 Arrive at the parking area.

5 Gold Branch Unit Trails

Located above the shores of Bull Sluice Lake, an impoundment of the Chattahoochee River created by construction of Morgan Falls Dam in 1904, Gold Branch is one of the less frequently visited units of the national recreation area. The unit is known for its network of upland and shoreline trails, and for its numerous vantage points for viewing waterfowl and wildlife along the lake and the river.

Start: Gold Branch Unit parking area off Lower Roswell Road
Distance: 4.2 miles with short lollipop entry and long circuit of interconnecting loops
Approximate hiking time: 2 to 3 hours
Elevation gain/loss: 150 feet
Trail surface: Hard-packed dirt, wooden steps
Lay of the land: Wetlands, lake and river shore, mixed hardwood and pine forest
Difficulty: Moderate to difficult due to distance, rocky terrain, and steep hills
Seasons: Year-round
Canine compatibility: Leashed dogs permitted

Land status: National Park Service
Fees and permits: Daily pass; annual pass available (all units)
Schedule: Open dawn to dark
Nearest town: Roswell
Maps: USGS Sandy Springs; maps also available from park website (maps are downloadable to tablet or smartphone with QR code and marked waypoints)
Trail contact: Chattahoochee River National Recreation Area, 1978 Island Ford Rd., Atlanta 30350; (678) 538-1200; www.nps.gov/chat

Finding the trailhead: Follow GA 400 north to Northridge Road (exit 6). At the traffic light, turn right (west) on Northridge to Roswell Road. Turn right (north) on Roswell and drive about 2.0 miles to the bridge over the Chattahoochee River. Cross and turn left (west) on Azalea Drive, passing Fulton County's Chattahoochee River Park with picnic areas, boat ramps, playgrounds, and a paved walking path. Turn left (south) on Willeo Road and follow it for 0.8 mile past the Chattahoochee Nature Center. A short distance ahead, Willeo Road takes a sharp left (south) and becomes Lower Roswell Road. The entrance to the Gold Branch Unit is about 0.6 mile ahead on the left (south). GPS: N33 59.056' / W84 23.115'

The Hike

One of the less frequently visited park units, Gold Branch offers glimpses of second-growth forest slowly recovering from intensive logging during the first half of the last century.

From the parking area, the blue-blazed trail descends past an information board and into the surrounding woods. At 0.2 mile the path crosses a footbridge over Gold Branch, a shallow stream that flows into Bull Sluice Lake. On the far side you will reach a marked trail intersection. Turn left and follow the slope of a ridge above the creek, ascending across a ravine on another narrow bridge. Continue to climb along the slope until the path reaches a level area featuring excellent views of Bull Sluice Lake, created by construction of Morgan Falls Dam.

Quiet trails in winter

At 0.5 mile you will reach a marked intersection. Turn sharply right, moderately ascending through a mixed hardwood forest to a ridgeline where the path follows a level course to another intersection at 0.9 mile. Turn left (the path to the right returns to the parking area), and begin a steady descent toward the lake on long switchbacks, reaching a marked intersection at 1.5 miles. At this point the trail bends sharply to the right and follows the shore of a small inlet. When you reach an intersection a short distance ahead, bear left, following the path to a wet stone crossing of a stream bottom, before ascending steeply on the opposite bank. The trail levels out and bends left, then right, following the banks of Bull Sluice Lake for the next half mile. Several vantage points offer excellent views of the lake and are superb points for observing waterfowl, especially during migratory seasons.

At 2.1 miles, reach a marked intersection. Follow the trail to the left and continue along the lakeshore. Crossing a streambed over a log bridge, begin traversing several stretches of exposed rock. The trail then bends away from the water and begins a winding, steady ascent of heavily wooded slopes— second-growth hardwoods and younger pines.

When constructed in 1904, Morgan Falls Dam provided hydroelectric power for Atlanta's electric streetcar system.

Merge with an old logging road at 3.1 miles. The path ascends for another quarter mile, past a signed intersection. Continue straight, climbing over a shallow ridge to another intersection at 3.7

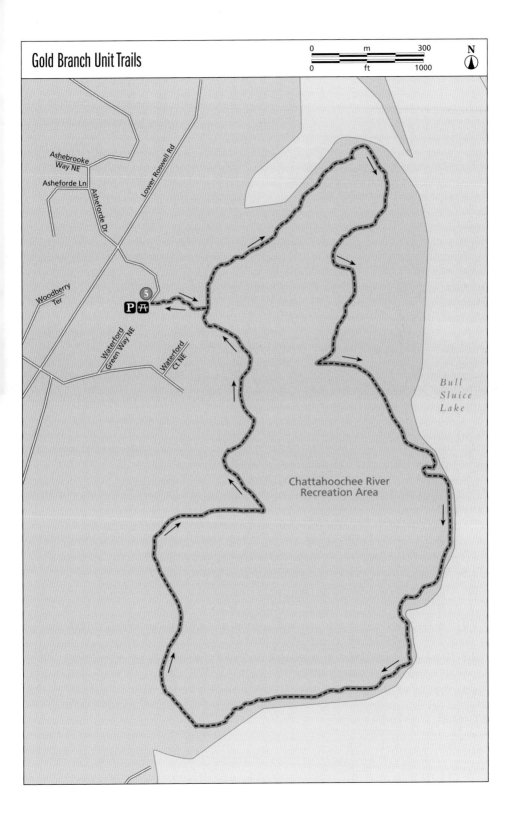

Gold Branch Unit Trails

0 m 300
0 ft 1000

N

Ashebrooke Way NE
Asheforde Ln
Asheforde Dr
Lower Roswell Rd
Woodberry Ter
Waterford Green Way NE
Waterford Ct NE

5
P 🏕

Chattahoochee River Recreation Area

Bull Sluice Lake

Bull Sluice Lake from the trail

miles. Turn left and quickly descend to the bridge over Gold Branch. From this point, retrace your steps to return to the parking area at 4.2 miles.

Miles and Directions

0.0   The trail descends from the information sign and pay kiosk by the parking area. GPS: N33 59.056' / W84 23.115'

0.5   At the location marker there is an excellent view of the lake. From here the trail turns right.

1.5   Turn right at the intersection above Bull Sluice Lake. GPS: N33 59.222' / W84 22.707'

2.1   At trail intersection, turn left and cross a creek, following the lakeshore. GPS: N33 58.601' / W84 22.678'

2.8   The trail bends away from the water and begins an ascent through the forest. GPS: N33 58.453' / W84 23.049'

3.7   At the intersection of two connecting trails, the main trail bends to the left and descends. GPS: N33 58.980' / W84 22.886'

4.2   You have returned to the starting point.

Nearby Attractions

Historic Roswell Village, 617 Atlanta St., Roswell 30075; (770) 640-3253; www.visit roswellga.com

6 Vickery Creek Unit Trails

Roswell King first glimpsed these wooded hills above the Chattahoochee River during a journey to the Dahlonega goldfields in the 1820s. King recognized that the terrain would someday be an ideal site for a textile mill. In 1839, following the Cherokee Removal, he established the village of Roswell on the recently ceded land. During the Civil War, the village's four mills and tannery were all destroyed by Union cavalry. Several were rebuilt, operating into the early 1900s. Today, vestiges of the mill village may still be seen in the cottages and commercial buildings of historic Roswell.

Start: Gravel parking area off Riverside Road
Distance: 5.3 miles consisting of a lollipop leading to a series of interconnecting loops. Extending the hike to view mill ruins, Vickery Creek Dam, Roswell Founders' Cemetery, and Roswell business district will add 2.0 miles.
Approximate hiking time: 2 to 3 hours
Elevation gain/loss: 168 feet
Trail surface: Compacted dirt, log steps
Lay of the land: Wooded, rolling hills and creek bottoms
Difficulty: Moderate due to distance and rolling terrain
Seasons: Year-round

Canine compatibility: Leashed dogs permitted
Land status: National Park Service
Fees and permits: Daily pass; annual pass available (all units)
Schedule: Open dawn to dark
Nearest town: Roswell
Maps: USGS Roswell; maps also available from the park website (maps are downloadable to tablet or smartphone with QR code and marked waypoints)
Trail contact: Chattahoochee River National Recreation Area, 1978 Island Ford Parkway, Atlanta 30350; (678) 538-1200; www.nps.gov/chat

Finding the trailhead: Drive north on GA 400 to Northridge Road (exit 6). Turn right (west) at the traffic light and follow Northridge 0.5 mile to Roswell Road. Turn right (north) and drive 1.7 miles, crossing the Chattahoochee River, to the intersection of Azalea Drive/Riverside Road. Turn right (east) on Riverside, then immediately left (north) at the signed entrance to the park. The trail begins at the far end of the gravel parking lot. GPS: N34 00.436' / W84 21.072'

The Hike

The trail ascends from the gravel parking area on a long switchback to the crest of a heavily wooded ridge before descending to an intersection at 0.7 mile. Continue straight (the path to the right exits the park) before bending left past another access trail intersection. At 1.0 mile, pass a loop trail entering from the left. Continue straight, past another trail intersection a short distance ahead, as the path climbs toward Grimes Bridge Road at 1.3 miles.

At a T intersection (the trail to the right leads to Grimes Bridge Road), turn left a short distance and then follow the trail to the right to reach the southern bank of Vickery Creek. Turn right along rolling slopes above the creek. At 1.9 miles, pass

Vickery Creek Falls and Dam

beneath a footbridge that crosses the creek to a parking area on Oxbo Road and then to Roswell's Waller Park.

Continue straight through thickets of mountain laurel as the path ascends, bending away from the creek, past a side trail exiting to the right. At 2.2 miles, turn left at another intersection and wind through an area of small clearings and second-growth

Trail through mixed forest above Vickery Creek

forest as the path closes a loop. Continue straight through an intersection at 2.6 miles and follow a meandering ridgeline. At a T intersection, turn right and retrace your steps a short distance before a right turn, following a lower ridge eastward.

Bear right at another T intersection and trek past a side trail on the left to another intersection bordered by a rail fence along a steep bluff above Vickery Creek. At 3.9

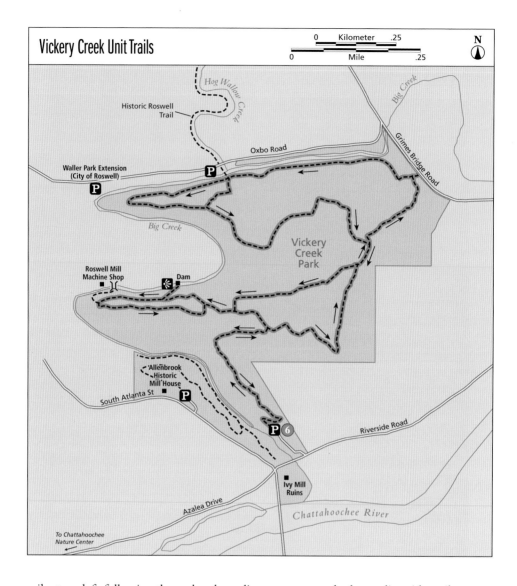

miles turn left, following the path a short distance to a steeply descending side trail on the right. This path leads to a viewpoint of Vickery Creek Dam. Retrace your steps back to the main trail and turn left. As the trail bends above the river, another side trail exits to the right and descends to a covered pedestrian bridge above the creek. The bridge provides access to trails on the north side of the creek and to historic downtown Roswell.

Continue on the main trail a short distance before turning left again and ascending along the path to an intersection at 3.4 miles. Bear left and follow the trail to a T intersection at 3.7 miles (the trail to the right leads steeply down to a linear trail along the creek). Bear right and retrace your steps past a previously hiked loop trail,

FLYING THE FRENCH FLAG

In July 1864, General William T. Sherman dispatched Union cavalry to Roswell to capture the mills that were supplying cloth to the Confederate army. As they approached, mill manager Theophile Roche, a French national, raised his country's flag atop the mill and claimed it to be French property. This so irritated Sherman that he gave orders for the mills to be burned and the workers sent north as prisoners of war. Sherman considered hanging Roche, but he somehow managed to escape the noose.

continuing straight to an intersection at 4.7 miles with the access trail leading back to the starting point. Turn right at the intersection, retracing your path across the ridge and down the long switchback to the gravel parking lot at 5.3 miles.

Miles and Directions

0.0 At the trailhead, note the old stone wall on the left along the creek, which is evidence of the Ivy Woolen Mill, erected in 1840s. GPS: N34 00.436' / W84 21.072'

0.5 Continue straight at the intersection, then the trail bears right with a moderate ascent over a ridge. GPS: N34 00.689' / W84 21.061'

0.7 At the T intersection, turn left.

1.3 After a left turn at the intersection with the access trail to Grimes Bridge Road, take trail to right. GPS: N34 01.030' / W84 20.638'

1.9 Cross beneath the Oxbo Road footbridge. GPS: N34 01.000' / W84 21.155'

2.2 Take a sharp right turn at the intersection and ascend away from the creek valley.

3.1 Turn right to complete the first loop, and make another right turn in 0.1 mile. GPS: N34 00.971' / W84 21.225'

4.0 Descend to the overlook of the Vickery Creek Dam. GPS: N34 00.763' / W84 21.466'

4.7 Complete the loop and turn right to retrace your steps. GPS: N34 00.657' / W84 21.111'

5.3 You have returned to the starting point.

Nearby Attractions

Roswell River Walk and Park, 203 Azalea Dr., Roswell 30076; (770) 641-3705; www.visitroswellga.com

Historic Roswell Village, 617 Atlanta St., Roswell 30075; (770) 641-3705; www.visit roswellga.com

7 Island Ford Unit Trails

Following removal of the Cherokee from northern Georgia, pioneers moved into this area, establishing the nearby town of Roswell on bluffs above the Chattahoochee and carving out farms along the waterway. There were few ferries across the river, so settlers crossed at shallow fords. One such site was Island Ford. When President Jimmy Carter created the Chattahoochee River National Recreation Area in 1978, this site included the former vacation home of Judge Samuel Hewett (c. 1930s). Today, the rustic log and stone structure serves as the national recreation area's headquarters and visitor center.

Start: Visitor center parking area
Distance: 6.3-mile circuit hike of interconnecting loops
Approximate hiking time: 3 to 4 hours
Elevation gain/loss: 190 feet
Trail surface: Mix of compacted soil and sandy floodplain
Lay of the land: River floodplain, upland slopes
Difficulty: Moderate due to distance and some steep terrain
Seasons: Year-round
Canine compatibility: Leashed dogs permitted

Land status: National Park Service
Fees and permits: Daily pass; annual pass available (all units)
Schedule: Dawn to dark
Nearest town: Roswell
Maps: USGS Chamblee; maps also available from park website (maps are downloadable to tablet or smartphone with QR code and marked waypoints)
Trail contact: Chattahoochee River National Recreation Area, 1978 Island Ford Parkway, Atlanta 30350; (678) 538-1200; www.nps .gov/chat

Finding the trailhead: Travel north on GA 400 to Northridge Road (exit 6). As you exit, remain in the right lane and cross the highway bridge. Turn right (north) at the first traffic light onto Dunwoody Place. Drive north for 0.6 mile and turn right (east) on Roberts Drive. Travel for 0.7 mile, crossing beneath GA 400, to Island Ford Parkway. Turn right (north) and follow the parkway for about 1 mile, turning left into the visitor center parking area. GPS: N33 59.232' / W84 19.497'

The Hike

From the visitor center parking area, descend the trail to the left of the building, and proceed to the floodplain trail beside a boat ramp and recreation field. Turn left and follow the path north along the river, crossing a footbridge at 0.2 mile. Continue straight (the path to the left returns to the parking lot) and enjoy panoramic views of the Chattahoochee as it winds along shallow, rocky shoals. This section of the river is especially popular with fly-fishers.

Reach an intersection by a large overhanging rock at 0.5 mile. The path to the left climbs the heavily wooded slopes back to the visitor center. Continue to follow the river, cross a footbridge, and go past another large rock outcrop. Reach another

Viewing Island Ford from trail

intersection at 0.7 mile. The path, ascending on steps to the left, may be used to shorten the loop. The river trail continues straight, past another upland trail, before it bends west at 0.8 mile and begins an ascent above Beech Creek.

Climb the heavily wooded slopes, following switchbacks and crossing two foot-bridges, and reach the north parking lot at 1.5 miles. Bear right and follow the trail across old Roberts Road and reenter the woods (note that this part of the trail is part of the Sandy Springs Trail System). Descend the slope on a series of switchbacks, crossing a ravine at 1.8 miles. Ascend along the slope and bear left. At an intermittent streambed, bend left and ascend across a ridge.

Descend the slope and across a bridge at 2.3 miles to the river bottom. Continue straight to a T intersection and bear right. At 2.9 miles, reach the end of the loop with an overlook of the river and highway bridge.

Turn right to begin the return, reaching the north parking area at 4.4 miles. Retrace your steps on the descent to a trail intersection at 4.8 miles. Turn right and ascend, bending left as you cross a ridge and begin a gradual descent, crossing

Fall color along the river at Island Ford

Summerbrook Creek on rocks before rejoining the river trail at 5.7 miles. Bear right, and retrace your steps for 0.3 mile before ascending the trail to the right, reaching a parking area.

Descend on steps across the park entrance road and reenter the woods to the right as the path follows the shore of a small pond. At 6.1 miles, cross a footbridge over a

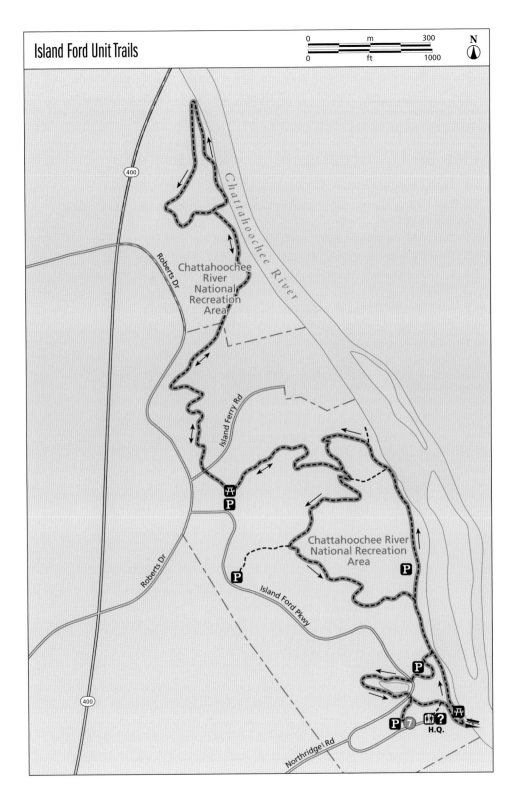

Island Ford Unit Trails

0   m   300
0   ft   1000

N

Chattahoochee River

400

Roberts Dr

Chattahoochee River National Recreation Area

Island Ferry Rd

Chattahoochee River National Recreation Area

Roberts Dr

Island Ford Pkwy

400

Northridge Rd

H.Q.

stream and climb steps as the trail follows the slope contour above the water. Turn left and continue east to complete the loop around the pond.

Recross the road and follow steps past a trail marker, reenter the woods, and descend to the river trail, passing a small stream, stonework, and an old pump house beside the visitor center. Turn right and climb the steps past a picnic pavilion and return to the starting point at 6.3 miles.

Miles and Directions

0.0 Begin at the visitor center parking area. GPS: N33 59.232' / W84 19.497'

0.5 Pass the large rock outcrop and continue straight at the intersection. GPS: N33 59.505' / W84 19.521'

0.9 Bear left on the trail as it ascends away from the water.

1.5 Reach the north parking area. GPS: N33 59.695' / W84 19.889'

2.9 Turn left at the end of the north loop by the GA 400 bridge. GPS: N34 00.367' / W84 19.932'

4.8 Turn right at the intersection and ascend the slope on a long switchback.

5.9 The trail takes you around a small pond. GPS: N33 59.325' / W84 19.519'

6.2 Cross the entrance road.

6.3 Return to the visitor center.

GREEN TIP
Go out of your way to avoid birds and animals that are mating or taking care of their young.

8 Jones Bridge Unit Trails

After settling on this land in 1819, James Martin ran a ferry across the Chattahoochee River for many years. His descendants, the Jones family, operated the ferry until it was replaced by the steel bridge in 1904. By the 1930s, the structure had deteriorated to a point where it was declared unsafe and abandoned. The remaining metal span of the bridge collapsed into the river in January 2018. Today, this unit of the Chattahoochee River National Recreation Area offers more than 7 miles of trails along floodplains and across ridges of upland mixed forest. Within the park is the Chattahoochee River Environmental Education Center (CREEC), a converted residence used for outdoor educational classes.

Start: Northern parking area by comfort station
Distance: 6.8 miles in two loops connected by a linear path
Approximate hiking time: 3 to 4 hours
Elevation gain/loss: 98 feet
Trail surface: Hard-packed dirt
Lay of the land: River floodplain and upland forest slopes
Difficulty: Moderate due to distance and hilly terrain
Seasons: Year-round
Canine compatibility: Leashed dogs permitted
Land status: National Park Service
Fees and permits: Daily pass; annual pass available (all units)

Schedule: Dawn to dark
Nearest towns: Midway between Roswell and Norcross
Maps: USGS Roswell; maps also available from park website (maps are downloadable to tablet or smartphone with QR code and marked waypoints)
Trail contact: Chattahoochee River National Recreation Area, 1978 Island Ford Rd., Atlanta 30350; (678) 538-1200; www.nps.gov/chat. Information on CREEC programs is available from park headquarters and CREEC Facebook page.

Finding the trailhead: From Atlanta, follow GA 400 north to Holcomb Bridge Road/GA 140 East (exit 7). Turn right (east) and follow Holcomb Bridge Road 4.2 miles to Barnwell Road. Turn left (north) and travel 1.2 miles to the park entrance. Turn right (east) and drive 1.0 mile to the northern parking area. GPS: N34 00.080' / W84 14.384'

The Hike

From the northern parking area, walk east past a comfort station and information kiosk to an intersection with the river trail (steps ahead provide a launching area for canoes, kayaks, and rafts). Turn left and follow the riverbank. At 0.3 mile, a short boardwalk on the right leads to a river observation platform. Continue north, traversing an area of exposed rock and crossing a footbridge to an open meadow with picnic tables. Just ahead, at 0.6 mile, are the remains of the old Jones Bridge (note the large houses and fencing that follows the park boundary only a few yards from the bridge).

Morning fog over river from floodplain trail

Cross the meadow and follow the trail as it reenters the woods on an ascent to a ridge. After crossing the crest, the path descends on a switchback to an old road, bearing left and returning to the northern parking area at 1.2 miles. Retrace your steps across the parking lot to the river trail and turn right, again following the floodplain through lush undergrowth and crossing a suspension bridge at 1.6 miles. Reach a boat ramp and satellite parking area in another 0.3 mile; reenter the woods across another bridge and continue to follow the riverbank.

At 2.2 miles, the trail bends away from the water and ascends to the right on switchbacks to a ridge crest. The path descends, at times steeply, across a gravel road. Ascend the slope and cross another footbridge, following the contour of the slope as you pass through a power-line corridor. Continue along the slope on a gradual descent.

Turn left and rapidly descend, reaching the riverbank at 2.8 miles. Follow the river for 0.5 mile to a trail intersection and bear left; continue along the water. At 3.7 miles, cross a footbridge and turn left at the intersection. Turn left and follow the water through an area of thick willow and river cane. The trail bears right, past an unblazed trail leading away to the left. Continue straight, crossing a meadow, and bear left on an old road at 4.0 miles.

Gnarled trees along floodplain trail

Follow the old road a short distance, entering the grounds of the Chattahoochee River Environmental Education Center (CREEC); note signs for the outdoor amphitheater, River Glen Pond, and other features. Turn right and cross an open field to follow the upland trail.

Jones Bridge Unit Trails

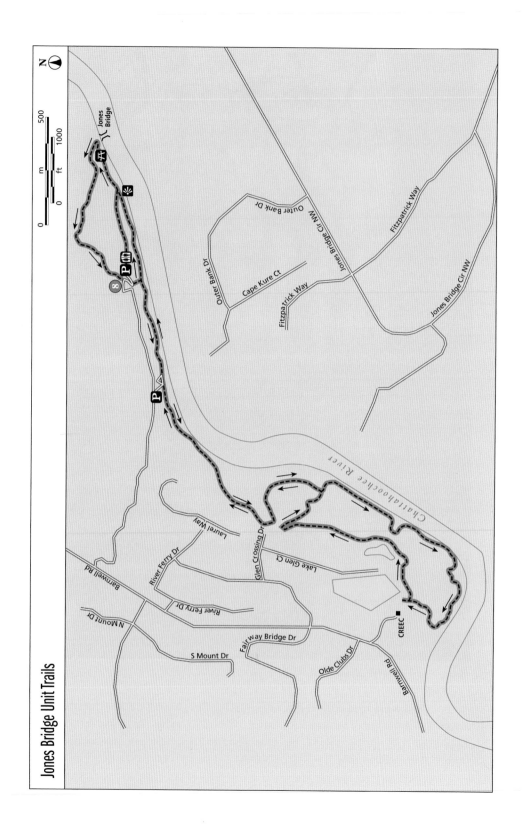

Reenter the woods below the pond. At the third trail marker (approximately 4.7 miles), turn left and steadily ascend the wooded slopes. Continue past another marker, ascending to the park boundary by Glen Crossing Road. Shortly before reaching the boundary posts, turn sharply right and descend on a lightly used path to the trail marker you passed on the outbound trek. At 5.4 miles, this closes the southern loop of the hike.

Retrace your steps, hiking beneath the power-line cut and across the gravel road, descending to the satellite parking area at 6.2 miles. Continue along the floodplain trail another half mile to reach your starting point at 6.8 miles.

Miles and Directions

0.0 Begin the hike at the north parking area. GPS: N34 00.080' / W84 14.384'

0.6 When you reach the Old Jones Bridge, you will see a homeowner has built a mansion on the property adjacent to the bridge.

1.2 Cross the parking area and turn right to continue on the river trail.

1.9 After crossing the footbridge, cross the satellite parking area and boat ramp to reenter the woods. GPS: N33 59.938' / W84 14.884'

2.2 Climb away from the river on a series of switchbacks and wooden steps to the crest of the ridge. GPS: N33 59.758' / W84 15.060'

2.8 The trail returns to the river.

3.7 Cross the footbridge at the signed intersection.

4.0 After crossing the meadow, follow the trail sign to the old road below the CREEC. GPS: N33 59.279' / W84 15.508'

4.8 Take a sharp right at the park boundary posts and descend to the return trail.

5.4 When you reach the signed intersection, retrace your steps back toward starting point.

6.2 Cross the satellite parking area.

6.8 The hike finishes at the north parking area.

Honorable Mentions

A. Powers Island Unit Trails, west of Cochran Shoals Unit on I-Parkway North

Located a short distance east of the Cochran Shoals Unit, the unit offers 3.6 miles of trails into upland slopes and along riverbanks to the ruins of the long-abandoned Puckett family residence (c. 1940s). The path also crosses a footbridge to Powers Island, where lightly used trails follow wetland areas to the northern tip of the island. To reach the unit, follow the directions for Cochran Shoals. The parking area, with a comfort station, is across the I-Parkway North bridge.

B. Johnson Ferry Unit Trails, 301 Johnson Ferry Rd. SE, Marietta, GA 30068

Located along the northern bank of the river, the unit preserves the site where William Johnson operated a ferry from the 1850s until 1879. The unit is divided into two sections, with the larger north of Johnson Ferry Road and the smaller south of the road. In the north, the Mulberry Trail traces a 2.5-mile lollipop loop across the broad floodplain and through surrounding lowland woods. To the south, a 0.3-mile linear trail follows the riverbank along an open field once used for polo matches. The large boat ramp in the north unit once bustled with summertime crowds when Johnson Ferry was the put-in point for commercial raft trips down the river.

To reach the unit, exit I-285 at Riverside Drive (exit 24) and drive north 2.3 miles to Johnson Ferry Road. Turn left (north) and cross the Chattahoochee River. The entrance to the northern part of the park is on the left. To reach the southern part of the park, turn left on Columns Drive. The trail difficulty is easy due to distance and modest elevation changes.

C. Medlock Bridge Unit Trails, 4690 Medlock Bridge Rd., Duluth, GA 30097

Tucked along a horseshoe bend of the river east of Peachtree Parkway in Alpharetta, the forty-three-acre unit offers 3 miles of trails along the water, across floodplains, and into the surrounding hills.

To reach the unit, travel north from I-285 on GA 400 to exit 10, Old Milton Parkway (GA 120). Turn right (east) on GA 120 and drive 6.2 miles to Medlock Bridge Road (GA 141). Turn right (south) on GA 141 and travel 4 miles. The entrance to the park is on the left. The trail difficulty is easy to moderate, with steep ascents into the hills west of the river.

Kennesaw Mountain National Battlefield Park

T ake the path across the Cheatham Hill Battlefield, and through woods where Union troops once waited to assault Rebel defenses. Like a silent sentinel, Kennesaw Mountain guarded the approach to Confederate-held Atlanta.

Cheatham Hill artillery battery

GREEN TIP
Don't take souvenirs home with you. This means natural materials such as plants, rocks, shells, and driftwood, as well as historic artifacts such as fossils and arrowheads.

9 Summit to Pigeon Hill Trails Loop

The 2,922-acre Kennesaw Mountain National Battlefield Park preserves the site of battles fought between determined Union and Confederate armies from June 22 to July 2, 1864. The summit and surrounding foothills provided strong defenses for Confederates protecting Atlanta. This trail climbs the northern slope of Kennesaw Mountain, past traces of rifle pits and restored artillery fortifications (please do not walk on these historic earthworks), before descending to the lower crest of Little Kennesaw Mountain. It then follows a rugged landscape to rock outcrops at Pigeon Hill. The trail returns along a service road (closed to automobiles) past the remnants of a 1930s Civilian Conservation Corps (CCC) camp.

Start: Behind the park visitor center.
Distance: 5.8-mile loop
Approximate hiking time: 3 to 4 hours
Elevation gain/loss: 696 feet
Trail surface: Mix of compacted soil, asphalt, and gravel
Lay of the land: Wooded mountain slopes and creek valleys
Difficulty: Moderate to strenuous due to distance and hilly terrain
Seasons: Year-round
Canine compatibility: Leashed dogs permitted

Land status: National Park Service
Fees and permits: Free
Schedule: Park trails open daily from dawn to dark; visitor center open daily from 8:30 a.m. to 5 p.m. (later during daylight saving time)
Nearest town: Marietta
Maps: USGS Marietta; maps also available from the visitor center and on the park website
Trail contact: Kennesaw Mountain National Battlefield Park, 900 Kennesaw Mountain Drive, Kennesaw 30152; (770) 427-4686; www.nps.gov/kemo

Finding the trailhead: Travel north on I-75 to Canton Street Connector (exit 267B). In 0.3 mile, turn right on Church Street Extension. Turn left in 0.6 mile on Old US 41 and follow it for 1.1 mile. Turn left on Stilesboro Road and the park entrance is on the left. There is also a small satellite parking area on Burnt Hickory Road. GPS: N33 58.982' / W84 34.722'

The Hike

Begin your hike behind the visitor center with a stop at the information board that provides details on the role of Kennesaw Mountain as vital wildlife habitat. Cross Kennesaw Mountain Drive and the Kennesaw Mountain Trail begins at the edge of the woods. The path gradually ascends a series of switchbacks to an intersection with the old gravel summit road, bending right and continuing along the old road before ascending again, at times steeply, to the Kennesaw Mountain summit parking area. Here the path follows the sidewalk a short distance before climbing stone steps to a large observation deck. During the leafless winter months, the deck offers a panoramic view of the 1864 route of the Western & Atlantic Railroad line, which the Union Army followed on its month-long march toward Atlanta. From the deck,

Rock outcrops on Pigeon Hill

continue climbing on an asphalt surface, past restored artillery fortifications, to a rock outcrop on the mountain summit at 1.0 mile.

From the peak, the Little Kennesaw Mountain Trail quickly and steeply descends along a rocky path to a crossing of Kennesaw Mountain Drive. After crossing, you will descend on several steps to a narrow path leading down to a saddle before climbing again to the summit of Little Kennesaw Mountain at 1.9 miles. Devoid of trees during the Civil War, this heavily wooded ridge was the site of Fort McBride.

From the crest of Little Kennesaw, the trail continues on a steep descent along rock- and root-studded slopes, following a series of long switchbacks to level and heavily wooded terrain. Pass the Little Kennesaw Cutoff trail before entering an area

A HEAVY LOAD

On the night of June 19, 1864, under cover of darkness, the Rebels hauled nine large cannons, and their caissons, up Little Kennesaw Mountain to reinforce Fort McBride located atop the ridge. Using ropes, they pulled the artillery up the steep, rock-strewn slopes by hand—one hundred men for each gun. As you stand atop the fortifications on Little Kennesaw, glance behind you and imagine the exhausted men straining to pull those heavy cannons to the summit.

Paved path to Kennesaw Mountain summit

of large boulders and rock outcrops dubbed "Pigeon Hill." As you pass among these stones, you may readily see why the Rebels considered this a nearly impregnable defensive position.

Descend along exposed rocks to a trail intersection and continue a short distance to an historical marker and photograph noting the nearby scene of bitter fighting between Missouri soldiers serving North and South—a poignant reminder that the Civil War often pitted neighbor against neighbor. Retrace your steps to the Pigeon Hill Cutoff trail intersection and turn right on a path connecting with the Camp Brumby Trail at 2.7 miles.

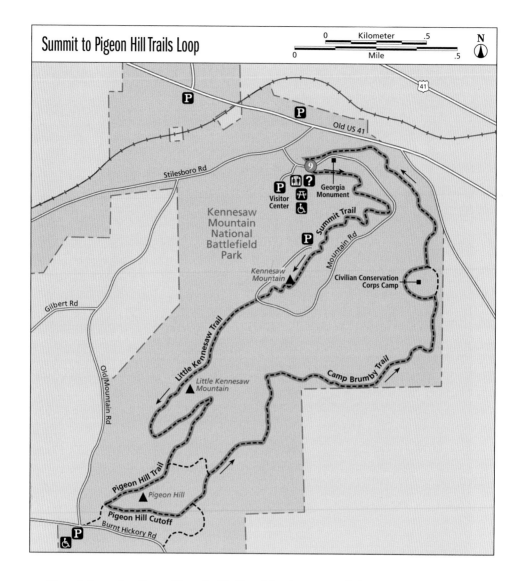

Turn left on the Camp Brumby Trail and begin your trek back toward the visitor center. The wide path follows the gentle grade of an old service road built by the Civilian Conservation Corps in the late 1930s. During that time, the men were working on the park's first facilities and infrastructure.

At 4.7 miles, the Camp Brumby Loop trail follows a short route through the site of the long-abandoned CCC Camp Brumby, where traces of old camp buildings and a parade ground are still evident. From the loop, return to the Brumby Trail and turn left, continuing to hike north. A short distance ahead, you will reach a trail fork. Turn left and enter the woods on a moderate ascent. Within a few yards, the path splits again. Take the right branch on a gentle descent as it bends to the left between

In addition to its history, Kennesaw Mountain National Battlefield Park provides important habitats for wildlife amid Atlanta's increasing urban development. The mountain's summit serves as a landmark on the Eastern Migratory Flyway; it's designated by the Audubon Society as an Important Bird Area (IBA) along the southern edge of the Blue Ridge Mountains.

Kennesaw Mountain Drive and a large open meadow on the return to the visitor center at 5.8 miles.

Miles and Directions

0.0 The trail begins across Kennesaw Mountain Drive south of the visitor center. GPS: N33 58.982' / W84 34.722'

0.2 The trail bears right onto the old park service summit road.

0.4 From the old road, the trail bends right and ascends steeply on narrow switchbacks to the summit parking area.

0.8 After a steady ascent, you reach the summit parking area and shuttle bus stop. The sidewalk to the left offers a panoramic view of Marietta and downtown Atlanta.

1.0 At the summit of Kennesaw Mountain is a USGS survey marker for 1,793 feet. GPS: N33 58.582' / W84 34.752'

1.6 Begin a steady ascent to Little Kennesaw Mountain.

1.9 At the summit of Little Kennesaw Mountain are the original earthworks of Fort McBride. GPS: N33 58.237' / W84 35.216'

2.5 Continue straight at the intersection of the Little Kennesaw Cutoff trail, which is a shortcut to the visitor center.

2.7 After descending, follow the loop trail to the left toward the Camp Brumby Trail. GPS: N33 57.871' / W84 35.530'

3.0 Turn left toward the visitor center at the Brumby trail intersection.

4.7 The trail reaches an open meadow and the site of a CCC camp established to develop the park facilities. Note the scattered ruins of camp structures. GPS: N33 58.521' / W84 34.210'

4.8 Take the left fork to the visitor center.

5.1 Follow the path to the right to a large field east of Kennesaw Mountain Drive.

5.8 Past a small thicket of trees, you will reach the visitor center.

Nearby Attractions

Historic Marietta Visitor Center, 4 Depot St., Marietta 30060; (770) 429-1115; www.mariettasquare.com

Southern Museum of Civil War and Locomotive History, 2829 Cherokee St., Kennesaw 30144; (770) 427-2117; www.southernmuseum.org

10 Cheatham Hill to Pigeon Hill Trails Loop

This section of the national battlefield park contains much evidence of the strong Rebel fortifications. Traces of earthworks may still be seen along the trails, and historical markers note the sites of several long-vanished structures that soldiers would have seen at the time of the fighting (please do not walk on the historic fortifications).

Start: Parking area off Cheatham Hill Drive, near Illinois Monument
Distance: 6.2-mile loop
Approximate hiking time: 3 hours
Elevation gain/loss: 158 feet
Trail surface: Compacted soil
Lay of the land: Rolling mix of woods and open meadows
Difficulty: Moderate due to distance and rolling terrain
Seasons: Year-round
Canine compatibility: Leashed dogs permitted

Land status: National Park Service
Fees and permits: Free
Schedule: Open dawn to dark; visitor center is open daily from 8:30 a.m. to 5 p.m. (later during daylight saving time
Nearest town: Marietta
Maps: USGS Marietta; maps also available at the visitor center and on the park website
Trail contact: Kennesaw Mountain National Battlefield Park, 900 Kennesaw Mountain Drive, Kennesaw 30152; (770) 427-4686; www.nps.gov/kemo

Finding the trailhead: Drive north on I-75 to GA 120/South Marietta Parkway (exit 263). Follow the sign for Marietta. Turn right (west) on GA 120 and drive 3.2 miles, crossing US 41, to Marietta. Pass beneath a railroad bridge and turn right (north) on Atlanta Highway/GA 360. At the second traffic light, turn left (west) on Whitlock Avenue (continuation of GA 120) and follow it for 3.1 miles to Cheatham Hill Drive. Turn left (south); the parking area will be about 0.5 mile ahead. GPS: N33 56.237' / W84 35.806'

The Hike

From the parking area, follow the trail southward a short distance, past original Rebel earthworks, to the large Illinois Monument, dedicated by Union veterans on the occasion of the battle's fiftieth anniversary in 1914. From the monument, descend a short distance past the preserved remains of a tunnel dug by Union troops in a failed attempt to blow up the Confederate fortifications. Immediately turn right and follow the Cease Fire Trail, which soon crosses a broad meadow. Beyond the open area, the trail reenters the woods and descends past the John Ward Connector trail to a crossing, at 0.8 mile, of Dallas Highway (GA 120) at the intersection with Cheatham Hill Drive. Cross to the north side of the highway and reenter the woods on Hardage Mill Trail, just west of the gated service road.

After a gentle climb, the trail begins a steady descent on several long switchbacks to Noses Creek, then follows the south bank of the stream to a wooden footbridge. Cross the bridge and immediately turn left, briefly following the north bank of the

Trail through meadow near Pigeon Hill

creek (a small marker notes the site of a mill that stood here in 1864) before bearing right and climbing, at times steeply, to a ridgeline above.

After ascending, the trail connects with the West Trail. Follow this path to the left as it continues on a gentle grade to an open meadow and the intersection with Burnt Hickory Road at 3.1 miles.

Cross the road and reenter the woods, following the trail signs to Pigeon Hill. After ascending along a rocky path, past an historical marker and photograph noting the site of fierce fighting between Missouri Federals and Rebels, turn right on the Pigeon Hill Cutoff trail and descend through thick woodlands to the Camp Brumby Trail (an old service road closed to automobiles).

Turn right on the Brumby Trail and follow it across Burnt Hickory Road at 3.9 miles. Descend a set of steps before climbing along switchbacks, past a sign noting the site of the Civil War–era New Salem Church.

The path traces a route along the crest of a wooded ridge before descending to a small meadow. After crossing the meadow, climb steeply into the woods on the far side. Following the slope, the trail descends again to an intersection with a connecting path linking the two trails. Continue on the Noses Creek Trail, and retrace your steps across the footbridge over Noses Creek at 4.9 miles. Continue straight as the path follows a gentle ascent along an old road toward Dallas Highway (GA 120).

After crossing the busy highway at the gated intersection, you may choose to retrace your steps on the footpath to the right of the road, or follow winding Cheatham Hill Drive back to the starting point at 6.2 miles.

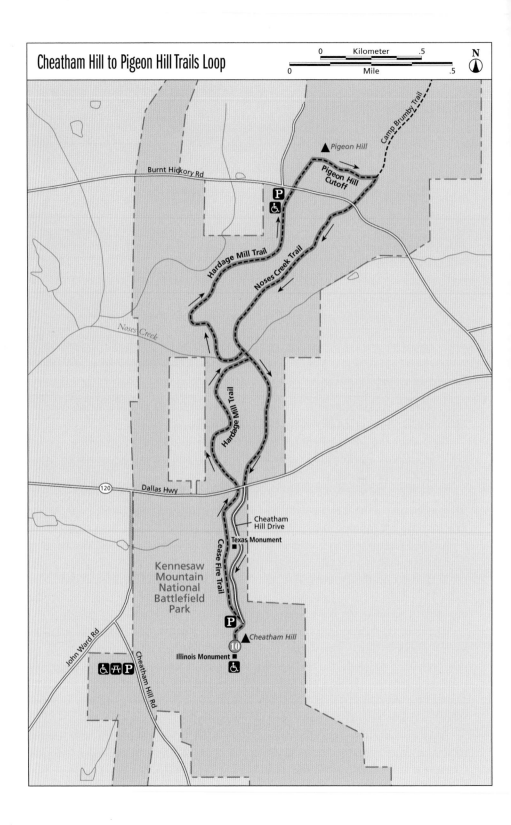

Cheatham Hill to Pigeon Hill Trails Loop

0   Kilometer   .5
0   Mile   .5

N

Pigeon Hill

Camp Brumby Trail

Burnt Hickory Rd

P

Pigeon Hill Cutoff

Hardage Mill Trail

Noses Creek Trail

Noses Creek

Hardage Mill Trail

120   Dallas Hwy

Cheatham Hill Drive

Texas Monument

Cease Fire Trail

Kennesaw Mountain National Battlefield Park

P

10   Cheatham Hill

Illinois Monument

John Ward Rd

Cheatham Hill Rd

P

Confederate earthworks near Cheatham Hill

Miles and Directions

0.0 Begin at the Cheatham Hill parking area and follow Cease Fire Trail. GPS: N33 56.237' / W84 35.806'

0.8 Cross Dallas Highway with care and reenter the woods on the Hardage Mill Trail. GPS: N33 56.738' / W84 35.830'

1.9 After descending, cross the footbridge over Noses Creek.

3.1 Cross Burnt Hickory Road and follow the trail signs to Pigeon Hill. GPS: N33 57.785' / W84 35.613'

3.2 Turn right on Pigeon Hill Cutoff trail, just past the Missouri marker.

3.9 Recross Burnt Hickory Road on Camp Brumby Trail. GPS: N33 57.730' / W84 35.291'

4.2 Cross a small meadow on the Noses Creek Trail.

4.9 Recross the footbridge over Noses Creek.

5.5 Cross Dallas Highway at the gated intersection.

6.2 Return to the Cheatham Hill parking area.

Judge Kenesaw Mountain Landis, first commissioner of Major League Baseball (appointed to clean up the infamous Black Sox scandal of 1919), was given the name by his father, Abraham Landis, who was a wounded veteran of the battle.

11 Cheatham Hill to Kolb Farm Trails Loop

This section traces a path across the Cheatham Hill Battlefield and through woods where Union troops once waited to assault the Rebel defenses. It descends across John Ward Creek before winding across forests and meadows to Powder Springs Road near the Kolb Farm, site of vicious fighting on June 22, 1864. The path then meanders through forests and shallow creek valleys on a return to the eastern side of Cheatham Hill. (Please do not walk on the historic earthworks.)

Start: Cheatham Hill parking area
Distance: 5.3-mile loop
Approximate hiking time: 3 hours
Elevation gain/loss: 168 feet
Trail surface: Compacted soil
Lay of the land: Mix of wooded slopes, bottomlands, and open meadows
Difficulty: Moderate due to distance and gently rolling terrain
Seasons: Year-round
Other trail users: Equestrians
Canine compatibility: Leashed dogs permitted

Land status: National Park Service
Fees and permits: Free
Schedule: Trails open dawn to dusk; visitor center open daily from 8:30 a.m. to 5 p.m.; later during daylight saving time
Nearest town: Marietta
Maps: USGS Marietta; maps also available at the visitor center and on the park website
Trail contact: Kennesaw Mountain National Battlefield Park, 900 Kennesaw Mountain Drive, Kennesaw 30152; (770) 427-4686; www.nps.gov/kemo

Finding the trailhead: From Atlanta, travel north on I-75 to South Marietta Parkway/GA 120 (exit 263). Follow exit sign toward Marietta and turn right (west) on GA 120 and drive 3.2 miles, crossing US 41, toward Marietta. After passing beneath railroad tracks, turn right (north) on Atlanta Highway/GA 360. Turn left (west) on Whitlock Avenue, a continuation of GA 120. Whitlock becomes Dallas Highway. After 3.9 miles, turn left (south) on Cheatham Hill Drive and proceed about a half mile to the parking area. There are satellite parking areas on Cheatham Hill Road and adjacent to the Kolb Farm off Powder Springs Road. GPS: N33 56.195' / W84 35.826'

The Hike

Some of the fiercest fighting during the Civil War's Georgia Campaign occurred along the route of this hike. Begin near the Illinois Monument (dedicated by Union veterans in 1914, the fiftieth anniversary of the battle), just below the original Rebel fortifications atop the summit of Cheatham Hill. The Cease Fire Trail descends and turns left. A short distance ahead you will reach the intersection of the unmarked Assault Trail. Turn right and continue downward across the northern edge of an open meadow and across a stream before ascending into woods on the other side. As you pass beneath the trees, imagine thousands of Union soldiers poised here for an attack across the open fields below.

Illinois Monument on Cheatham Hill

The trail crosses the edge of another meadow before reaching Cheatham Hill Road and a satellite parking area at 0.7 mile. Cross the parking area and reenter the woods on the Kolb Farm West Trail, a gentle climb followed by a steady descent. Skirt the edge of a meadow (be alert to deer and wild turkey often spotted here) and continue a downward trek to a wetlands area along John Ward Creek.

Grave of Union soldier on trail below Cheatham Hill

At 1.7 miles, cross a footbridge and hike through an open meadow, bending left for an easy climb, then turning right and reentering the woods. As you approach Powder Springs Road, note a bamboo thicket along the left side of the trail. At 2.9 miles, you will reach the trail's intersection with Cheatham Hill Road. If you wish, you may cross busy Powder Springs Road to view the restored Kolb Farm (not open to the public) before returning to Cheatham Hill Road and continuing on the Kolb Farm East Trail.

The path crosses a meadow and reenters the woods, following rolling terrain as it bends north. Along the route, the path passes a number of houses built along the park boundaries. After a descent on switchbacks and across an intermittent stream, the trail ascends, bearing left, to a level course along the edge of a small stream. After descending again to a footbridge, a horse trail joins from the left.

AN ACT OF COMPASSION

At the peak of the fighting at Cheatham Hill, artillery shells set the surrounding woods ablaze, threatening many gravely wounded Union soldiers. Confederate Colonel W. H. Martin raised a flag of truce and, for a few minutes, men from both armies worked side by side to move the dead and injured out of the path of the flames.

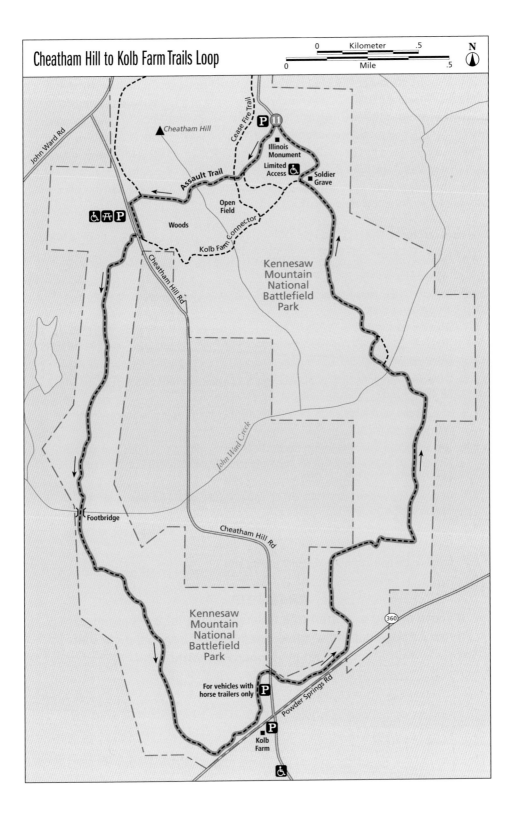

Cheatham Hill to Kolb Farm Trails Loop

0 Kilometer .5

0 Mile .5

N

Cheatham Hill

Cease Fire Trail

P 11

Illinois Monument

Limited Access

Soldier Grave

Assault Trail

Open Field

Woods

Kolb Farm Connector

Kennesaw Mountain National Battlefield Park

John Ward Rd

Cheatham Hill Rd

John Ward Creek

Footbridge

Cheatham Hill Rd

Kennesaw Mountain National Battlefield Park

360

For vehicles with horse trailers only

P

Powder Springs Rd

P Kolb Farm

Once across the bridge, the trail widens and continues a gentle rise as it approaches the Cheatham Hill area. You will reach a three-way intersection at 5.0 miles. Bear left and follow the Kolb Farm Connector trail. A short distance ahead, turn right and climb the Cheatham Hill Trail past the preserved grave of a Union soldier found here by Civilian Conservation Corps (CCC) workers in 1938. While the grave remains marked as "unknown," he was identified in 2009 by a park volunteer following years of painstaking research. The soldier was Private Mark Carr of the 34th Illinois infantry. He was killed on June 27, 1864, during the assault on Cheatham Hill, and his body was hidden from view for more than seventy years. Continue past the Illinois Monument to complete the loop at 5.3 miles.

Miles and Directions

0.0 From the Cheatham Hill parking area, follow the Cease Fire Trail south past restored fortifications. GPS: N33 56.195' / W84 35.826'

0.2 Descend on the unmarked Assault Trail at the northern edge of the open field and cross bridges over a stream.

0.7 Cross the parking area on Cheatham Hill Road and reenter the woods on the Kolb Farm West Trail.

1.3 Follow the path along the edge of a large clearing. GPS: N33 55.563' / W84 36.357'

1.7 Cross a footbridge over John Ward Creek and enter a meadow. GPS: N33 55.190' / W84 36.429'

1.9 Bear left and cross a stream on a footbridge, then bear to the right on an ascent along the edge of the woods.

2.9 Take a right turn and cross Powder Springs Road to view the old Kolb farmhouse. Retrace your steps and cross Cheatham Hill Road to reenter the woods on the Kolb Farm East Trail. GPS: N33 54.774' / W84 35.668'

4.2 Bear left at the signed intersection and ascend along the edge of the slope. GPS: N33 55.508' / W84 35.364'

5.0 Bear left at the intersection of Kolb Farm Connector trail. The side trail is a shortcut to the Cheatham Hill parking area.

5.3 Conclude the hike at the Cheatham Hill parking area.

GREEN TIP

If you're driving to or from the trailhead, don't let any passenger throw garbage out the window. Keep a small bag in the car that you can empty properly at home.

12 Piedmont National Wildlife Refuge Trails

At first glance, the Piedmont National Wildlife Refuge appears as a natural landscape. In fact, the heavily wooded hills and valleys represent the culmination of years of effort to restore land devastated by ruinous agriculture. During the Depression, submarginal lands like these were purchased by the federal government, retired from farming, and science-based restoration efforts initiated. It was through this initiative that the 35,000-acre Piedmont National Wildlife Refuge was established in 1939 by the federal Resettlement Administration. Today, the refuge is home to many wildlife species, including more than 200 kinds of birds, and is testimony to the value of preserving and restoring the natural heritage of the Southern Piedmont.

Start: Parking area by Red-Cockaded Woodpecker and Allison Lake trailheads
Distance: 5.1-mile loops with connecting linear trail
Approximate hiking time: 3 hours
Elevation gain/loss: 184 feet
Trail surface: Compacted soil
Lay of the land: Rolling wooded hills, lowland creek valleys, and floodplains
Difficulty: Moderate
Seasons: Year-round
Canine compatibility: Leashed dogs permitted
Land status: United States Fish and Wildlife Service

Fees and permits: Free
Schedule: Trails open daily during daylight hours; closed on quota hunting days in fall and spring; visitor center open 8 a.m. to 5 p.m. Mon through Fri when staff is available.
Nearest towns: Forsyth, Juliette, and Round Oak
Maps: USGS Hillsboro and Berner; trail maps also available from website or at the visitor center
Trail contact: Piedmont National Wildlife Refuge, 718 Juliette Rd., Round Oak 31038; (478) 986-5441; www.fws.gov/piedmont

Finding the trailhead: Drive south on I-75 to the Forsyth exit on Juliette Road (exit 186). Turn left (east) on Juliette Road for 9.2 miles, passing the village of Juliette near the Ocmulgee River. Cross the river and continue east on Round Oak–Juliette Road for 3.5 miles to the intersection of Jarrell Plantation Road. Bear left (east) and continue on Round Oak–Juliette Road for another 4.3 miles. The entrance road leading to the visitor center and Allison Lake parking area will be on the left (north). Turn and follow the entrance road for about a half mile to the intersection with the visitor center driveway; continue straight for another quarter mile to the trail's parking area. GPS: N33.06.852' / W83.41.103'

The Hike

If you arrive at the Piedmont Wildlife Refuge during visitor center operating hours, take a few minutes to tour the exhibits, learn the natural and human history of the area, and pick up maps and guides to refuge trails and wildlife. You may begin the hike from the visitor center by following either the Creek or Pine Trails, which connect

Pines along Red-Cockaded Woodpecker Trail

with other refuge trails. The hike described below begins at the information kiosk near the Allison Lake parking area.

Begin your exploration with a trek on the 2.9-mile Red-Cockaded Woodpecker Trail, which descends from the parking area along a paved road to an observation deck on Allison Lake. Cross the earthen dam and go up an old service road. At 0.3 mile, a marker on the left notes the head of the Red-Cockaded Woodpecker Trail. Follow the trail across a ridge and descend to a footbridge over an intermittent stream before climbing toward the north.

At 0.7 mile, the path reaches a ridge and intersection of the Red-Cockaded Woodpecker Trail loop. Continue straight on a gentle descent through pine-shaded

Piedmont National Wildlife Refuge Trails

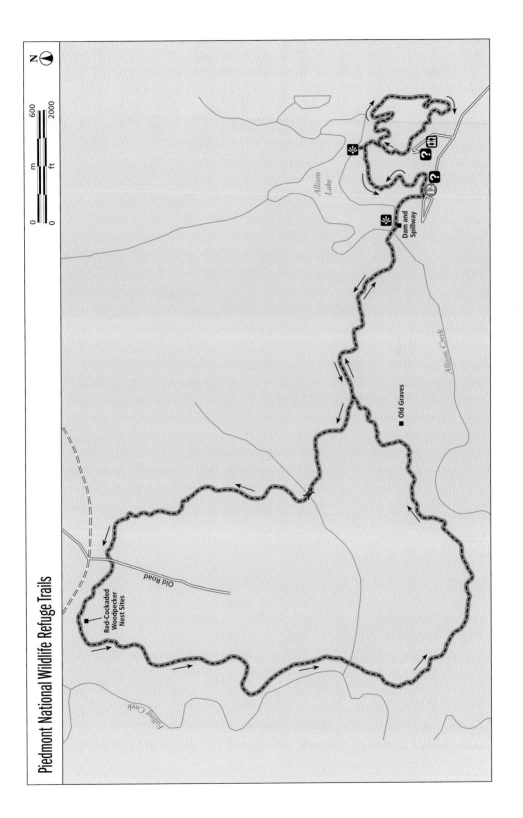

N

0   300   600   m
0   2000   ft

Balling Creek

Red-Cockaded Woodpecker Nest Sites

Old Road

Old Graves

Allison Lake

Dam and Spillway

Allison Creek

Red-cockaded woodpecker nest sites along Red-Cockaded Woodpecker Trail

slopes to another bridge and an ascent through a meadow. At 1.0 mile, the trail bends west and parallels a service road. Cross another service road before descending again through a broader valley, reaching a concentration of woodpecker nest sites at 1.5 miles. If you visit during peak nesting season (April through June), you may wish to linger here for a chance to spot the reclusive birds.

Bear sharply left and descend to a wet stream crossing before climbing a ridge and fording another small creek. Here, the path parallels Falling Creek for about a quarter mile before bending left and descending to the Allison Creek floodplain. After crossing the plain, climb away from the creek and into the wooded hills. At 2.3 miles the trail passes to the left of the graves of early settlers as it ascends to an old farm road that closes the trail loop at 2.5 miles. Turn right and retrace your steps to the dam and back to the parking area at 3.0 miles.

Continue your hike by following the Allison Lake Trail as it descends from the information kiosk, tracing the slope downward to the south before crossing a creek

RED-COCKADED WOODPECKER

The refuge's mature longleaf pine ecosystem has fostered restoration of the nest sites for the endangered red-cockaded woodpecker. These rare birds, once numbering in the millions across piedmont forests, are making a carefully monitored revival at the Piedmont National Wildlife Refuge. Naturalists and birding enthusiasts come from across the country to glimpse these reclusive creatures in their nest trees (marked by horizontal white blazes on tree trunks) along the refuge's Red-Cockaded Woodpecker Trail.

and ascending to a footbridge over a ravine. The path bends right, crosses a second bridge, and follows the slope before bearing east above Allison Lake. After traversing a steeper slope with several log steps, the path crests a ridge and descends over another footbridge toward the small lake. At 0.3 mile, an intersecting side trail leads down to an observation deck overlooking the lake.

From the intersection, the path turns right and climbs steadily to the Creek Trail and Pine Trail intersection at 0.5 mile. Turn left on the Creek Trail, descending on several switchbacks to a floodplain at 1.0 mile before bending right and climbing past rock outcrops to the Pine Trail at 1.3 miles. A short path to the left leads about 200 yards to the refuge visitor center.

Continue on the Pine Trail as it follows the ridge before descending to the Allison Lake and Creek Trails intersection at 1.8 miles. From that point, retrace your steps on the Allison Lake Trail to the parking area at 2.1 miles. A hike of the combined Red-Cockaded Woodpecker, Allison Lake, Creek, and Pine Trails is 5.1 miles.

Miles and Directions

0.0 Begin the hike at the information kiosk near the Allison Lake parking area. GPS: N33 06.852' / W83 41.103'

0.3 Look for the sign showing where the Red-Cockaded Woodpecker Trail exits the old service road. GPS: N33 06.972' / W83 41.307'

0.7 Continue straight at the intersection of the Red-Cockaded Woodpecker Trail loop. GPS: N33 07.024' / W83 41.632'

1.5 Pause and note the concentration of woodpecker nest sites. GPS: N33 07.014' / W83 42.052'

2.3 About 50 yards to the right are old grave sites of pioneers.

2.5 Turn right at the end of the Red-Cockaded Woodpecker Trail loop and return to the dam.

3.0 Return to the parking area and descend south on the Allison Lake Trail.

3.3 Enjoy the observation platform overlooking Allison Lake. GPS: N33 06.984' / W83 40.919'

3.5 At the intersection of the Creek Trail and Pine Trail, take a left turn and follow the Creek Trail.

4.0 Cross the fern-covered floodplain south of Allison Lake.

4.3 Continue straight at the intersection of Pine Trail and the visitor center access trail. GPS: N33 06.736' / W83 40.712'

4.8 When you reach the connection of Pine, Creek, and Allison Lake Trails, follow the Allison Lake Trail to return to the parking area.

5.1 You have reached the trailhead.

Nearby Attractions

Jarrell Plantation State Historic Site, 711 Jarrell Plantation Rd., Juliette 31046; (478) 986-5172; www.gastateparks.org/jarrellplantation

Rum Creek Wildlife Management Area, 116 Rum Creek Dr., 3 miles east of I-75; www.georgiawildlife.com/rum-creek-wma

US Army Corps of Engineers

Buford Dam was authorized by Congress in 1946 as part of a nationwide effort to improve flood control and to develop waterways. Work began on the dam in 1950 and was completed in 1957. Seven hundred families were relocated to make way for the 38,000-acre lake. While most buildings were removed, extended drought conditions have revealed ghostly skeletons of hundreds of long-submerged trees and debris.

Boardwalk trail through floodplain area

GREEN TIP

Consider the packaging of any products you bring with you. It's best to properly dispose of packaging at home before you hike. If you're on the trail, pack it out with you.

13 Laurel Ridge Trail on Lake Sidney Lanier

Nestled along upland slopes and wetlands of the Appalachian foothills adjacent to Lake Lanier's Buford Dam, Laurel Ridge Trail offers a glimpse of the landscape before the massive lake was completed by the US Army Corps of Engineers in 1957. Featuring more than 700 miles of shoreline, the multipurpose lake offers access to parks, picnic areas, and boating facilities. A portion of the trail below the dam follows the course of the Chattahoochee River as it flows from the lake toward Atlanta.

Start: Parking area on Buford Dam Road, just east of the dam in Lower Overlook Park

Distance: 3.8-mile loop

Approximate hiking time: 3 hours

Elevation gain/loss: 256 feet

Trail surface: Hard-packed dirt, some paved stretches, steps

Lay of the land: Upland slopes, bottomlands, lakeshore, riverbank

Difficulty: Moderate to strenuous

Seasons: Year-round

Canine compatibility: Dogs not permitted

Land status: US Army Corps of Engineers

Fees and permits: Free

Schedule: Open daily during daylight hours. Park hours change during different seasons and are posted at the entrance.

Nearest towns: Cumming and Buford

Maps: USGS Buford Dam; trail map also available from the corps of engineers website

Trail contact: US Army Corps of Engineers, Lake Lanier Management Office, 1050 Buford Dam Rd., Buford 30518; (770) 945-9531; http://www.sam.usace.army.mil/Missions/Civil-Works/Recreation/Lake-Sidney-Lanier/

Finding the trailhead: Drive north on I-85 to Lawrenceville-Suwanee Road/GA 317 (exit 111). Turn left (west) at the ramp and follow GA 317 for 2.1 miles to Buford Highway/US 23. Continue straight on Suwanee-Buford Dam Road (the name will change to Suwanee Dam Road) for 7.4 miles. Turn left (west) on Buford Dam Road for 0.4 mile and turn right (north) into the Lower Overlook Park parking area.

From GA 400, travel east on Buford Highway/GA 20 (exit 14) to Market Place Boulevard and turn left (north). Drive 0.6 mile and turn right (east) on Buford Dam Road. Travel 5.2 miles, across Buford Dam, and turn left (north) to the Lower Overlook Park parking area. GPS: N34 09.536' / W84 04.212'

The Hike

From the Lower Overlook Park parking area, follow the concrete path behind the comfort station, descending a shallow ravine before climbing up to Buford Dam Road. Cross and ascend a dirt path to the right, past the Upper Overlook Park picnic shelters. A glance to the right provides a panoramic view of Buford Dam. Descend to a second overlook platform offering winter views of the dam.

Continue descending and follow the steps to Power House Road at 0.5 mile. Cross the road and descend again to the eastern banks of the Chattahoochee River

Hiker on trail near Lake Sidney Lanier inlet above Buford Dam

where it flows from Lake Lanier. Note that the river rises rapidly (as much as 11 feet) during water releases, so be alert to warning whistles if you are on or near the river.

Follow a wooden bridge as you continue along the floodplain. A short distance ahead, a boardwalk crosses the river to Lower Pool Park, with a ramp for launching kayaks, canoes, and rafts. Several vantage points offer a panoramic view of the 2,360-foot-long dam that rises nearly 200 feet above the river.

At 0.9 mile, the trail bends sharply left and ascends from the floodplain into the surrounding woodlands. The climb is gradual to a small footbridge over a stream; it ascends more steeply on switchbacks, reaching a crossing of Buford Dam Road at 1.5 miles.

Laurel Ridge Trail on Lake Sidney Lanier

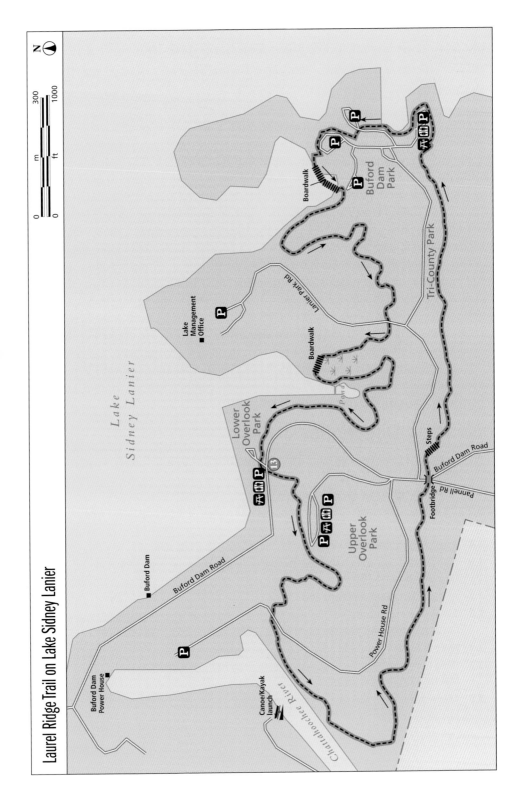

Lake Sidney Lanier

Buford Dam

Buford Dam Road

Buford Dam Power House

Canoe/Kayak launch

Chattahoochee River

Power House Rd

Upper Overlook Park

Lower Overlook Park

Lake Management Office

Pond

Boardwalk

Boardwalk

Lanier Park Rd

Tri-County Park

Buford Dam Park

Steps

Footbridge

Pannell Rd

Buford Dam Road

N

m
ft
0   300
0   1000

Lake Sidney Lanier is named for Georgia-born Sidney Lanier (1842–1881), lawyer, scholar, and poet best known for his works "The Song of the Chattahoochee," "Sunrise," and "The Marshes of Glynn."

After crossing, the path immediately descends a series of steps and reenters an upland forest. The path follows a gentle descent before crossing a power-line corridor and dropping more steeply into the woods on the far side. The trail follows a boardwalk through lush, fern-filled wetlands before it crosses a narrow service road at 2.2 miles. A short distance ahead, the trail bends right and enters a playground and picnic area in Buford Dam Park. Follow trail signs along the sidewalk, turning left and descending past two group shelters above the lake. The path follows a short switchback past a side trail to an overlook and crosses a cove on an elevated footbridge.

The trail ascends to the right, across another picnic area at 2.7 miles. Follow signs pointing left as the path passes a comfort station, then bends right on steps, crossing another elevated footbridge to the left. A steep ascent on the far side leads past a paved parking area and reenters the woods on a pine-shaded ridge with wide views of the lake. The path bends left and descends along switchbacks to a road crossing, then descends to a series of boardwalks that meander through a wetlands area.

The path bends sharply left along a small pond before ascending again at 3.2 miles. After a moderate climb, the trail follows the slope contour beneath Buford Dam Road on its return to the starting point.

Miles and Directions

0.0 Begin at the Lower Overlook Park parking area east of Buford Dam. GPS: N34 09.536' / W84 04.212'

0.6 After crossing the road the trail descends.

0.9 The wetlands trail bends sharply left and begins an ascent. GPS: N34 09.347' / W84 04.710'

1.4 A footbridge crosses the stream. Benches are available for a rest stop.

1.5 After crossing the Buford Dam Road, turn right and walk down the steps. GPS: N34 09.279' / W84 04.263'

2.2 A boardwalk crosses a wetland area.

2.3 Turn right to enter the Buford Dam Park playground and picnic area with restrooms. Follow the signs and turn left past two picnic shelters. GPS: N34 09.360' / W84 03.670'

2.7 Arrive at another picnic and playground area with restrooms.

3.2 Cross Lanier Park Road and descend on steps to wetlands area with boardwalks. GPS: N34 09.345' / W84 04.030'

3.8 After a steady climb, you return to the starting point.

Georgia Department of Natural Resources

Georgia State Parks and Historic Sites

Sweetwater Creek State Park preserves the ghostly ruins of the historic New Manchester Mill, destroyed by Union Cavalry on July 9, 1864. Before it was burned, the five-story New Manchester Mill was the tallest structure in the Atlanta area.

14 Pickett's Mill State Historic Site Trails

During the spring of 1864, Union General William T. Sherman led his troops into Georgia to engage the Rebel army and capture Atlanta. In his reports, Sherman made little mention of the May 27 fight at Pickett's Mill. The likely reason is that, among a string of victories, the battle was a stunning defeat brought about by poor field command and misunderstanding of the site's terrain. The site remained virtually unchanged in the decades after the war and is today considered among the best preserved Civil War battlefields in the nation.

Start: Behind the visitor center building
Distance: 5.4 miles of interconnecting loops
Approximate hiking time: 3 to 4 hours
Elevation gain/loss: 175 feet
Trail surface: Compacted soil
Lay of the land: Rolling descent from visitor center to banks of Pumpkinvine Creek
Difficulty: Easy to moderate
Seasons: Year-round
Canine compatibility: Leashed dogs permitted
Land status: Georgia State Parks and Historic Sites

Fees and permits: Admission fee is levied (youth and senior discounts available)
Schedule: Open 9 a.m. to 5 p.m. Thurs through Sat
Nearest town: Dallas
Maps: USGS Dallas; trail guides are available for purchase at the visitor center
Trail contact: Pickett's Mill Battlefield Historic Site, 4432 Mount Tabor Church Rd., Dallas 30157; (770) 443-7850; www.gastateparks .org/pickettsmillbattlefield

Finding the trailhead: Drive north on I-75 to the Canton Road Connector (exit 267B). Travel south to Church Street Extension and turn right, following it for 0.6 mile to Old US 41 and turn left. Drive 1.2 miles to Stilesboro Road and turn left, passing the main entrance to Kennesaw Mountain National Battlefield Park. Cross Barrett Parkway, and continue straight. In 3.3 miles, turn left on Kennesaw Due West Road. In 3.0 miles, continue straight on Due West Road. Travel 4.8 miles and turn left on Hiram Acworth Highway (GA 92), and in 0.1 mile turn right on the continuation of Due West Road. In 1.8 miles, turn right on Mount Tabor Church Road; the park entrance will be 0.2 mile ahead on the right. GPS: N33 58.437' / W84 45.548'

The Hike

From the rear entrance of the visitor center, descend steps and turn left on the Blue Trail. At 0.1 mile, bear right on the White Trail (an old farm road) and gently descend past a meadow (this was a wheat field at the time of the battle). The path forks; go left at 0.3 mile and you will meander through a wooded area. At the intersection with a closed trail, bear right and continue past fading remains of Union earthworks to the right of the path.

Old farm road through the battlefield

Follow the White Trail as it descends to the intersection of the Red and Blue Trails. Turn left on the Red/Blue Trail and continue down along the contour of a wooded slope, passing the edge of a meadow that was once a wheat field.

At 1.1 miles, reach the intersection with the Brand House Trail (marked with white blazes surrounding a B). Turn left and descend to a bridge across Pumpkinvine Creek (known as Pickett's Mill Creek in 1864). Cross the bridge and bear left, following the creek. Bear right and ascend away from the creek on an old farm road, reaching a level area at 1.6 miles and a marker noting the site of the Brand family house that was destroyed during the battle.

Split rail on edge of cornfield

The trail climbs a short distance to a sharp right turn and a steady descent along the heavily wooded slopes. Note the sites of Union and Confederate rifle pits along the right side of the trail during the descent. The trail descends steeply on switchbacks and reaches the footbridge at 2.3 miles. Cross the bridge and retrace your steps to the intersection with the Red/Blue Trail and continue descending to a bridge across a stream. Turn left on the Red/Blue Trail and in a short distance you reach the site of Pickett's Mill at 2.5 miles. Note the stacked stone foundations are the only remnants

DARK STORIES

A topographical engineer on Union Gen. William B. Hazen's staff at Pickett's Mill was twenty-two-year-old Lieutenant Ambrose Bierce. Bierce drew battlefield maps and conducted reconnaissance during the height of the battle. He would be gravely wounded at the Battle of Kennesaw Mountain a few weeks later. During his wartime service, Bierce began to write of his experiences but did not begin his career as a journalist until several years after the war. He is considered among the finest short-story writers of the nineteenth century, and many believe the dark nature of his stories, including "The Crime at Pickett's Mill," arose from his traumatic experiences during the Civil War.

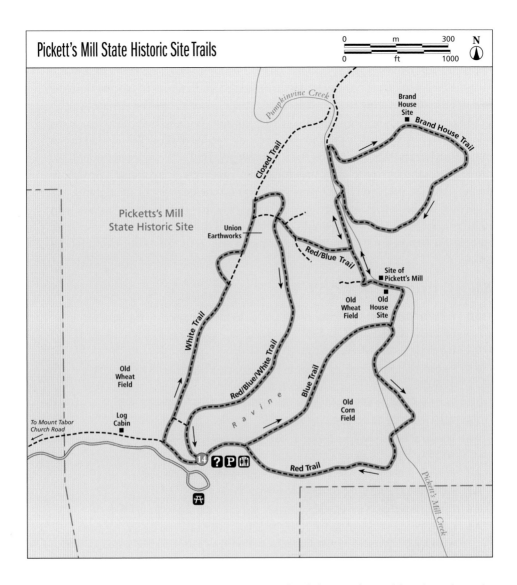

Pickett's Mill State Historic Site Trails

0   m   300

0   ft   1000

N

Pumpkinvine Creek

Brand House Site

Brand House Trail

Closed Trail

Picketts's Mill State Historic Site

Union Earthworks

Red/Blue Trail

Site of Pickett's Mill

Old Wheat Field

Old House Site

White Trail

Old Wheat Field

Red/Blue/White Trail

Blue Trail

Old Corn Field

Log Cabin

To Mount Tabor Church Road

R a v i n e

14 ? P

Red Trail

Pickett's Mill Creek

of the mill that was nearly destroyed during the fighting. The trail bends to the right and ascends past the site of the long-vanished miller's home and well.

At 2.7 miles, turn left on the Red Trail and descend along the slopes above the creek. Soon you cross a short footbridge to the opposite bank and wind through the wooded hills. A short distance ahead, cross a second bridge and ascend toward the edge of a meadow that was a cornfield in 1864. Bear left and continue to climb the moderately steep wooded slope. At 3.6 miles, turn left on the Red Trail (also old farm road), and follow it on a rolling, gentle ascent to an intersection with the Blue Trail, a short distance from the visitor center.

Turn right on the Blue Trail and follow the upper edge of a steep ravine that was a site of fierce fighting during the battle. Follow the trail as it winds along the slopes just above the deepest part of the ravine. Glance down to the ravine below and imagine Rebel soldiers pouring deadly fire into the Union troops advancing from the woods beyond the ravine to your left.

After retracing your steps past the old mill site and climbing along the edge of the wheat field, you will reach the intersection with the Red/Blue/White Trail at 4.5 miles. Turn left and descend on the Red/Blue/White Trail as it continues through the ravine where the Union soldiers, marching from your right, were trapped. At various points along the path, you might pause to reflect on the brutality of the fighting.

Reach the Blue Trail intersection at 5.2 miles. You may turn right and retrace your route past the White Trail to the old Leverett Farm Road Trail to see a reconstructed antebellum farmhouse (0.2-mile round-trip), or return to the visitor center at 5.4 miles.

Miles and Directions

0.0 From the deck behind the visitor center, turn left for a short distance to the White Trail. GPS: N33.58.437' / W84 45.548'

0.3 The trail forks left from the old road.

0.6 Beyond the Union earthworks the White Trail bends right. GPS: N33 58.872' / W84 45.405'

1.1 Reach intersection with Brand House Trail. GPS: N33 59.038' / W84 45.545'

1.6 Tablet marks site of the Brand House.

2.5 The site of Pickett's Mill is adjacent to Pumpkinvine Creek. GPS: N33 58.696' / W84 45.160'

2.7 Bear left on the Red Trail as it descends along the slope above the creek.

3.2 At the eastern edge of the cornfield, bear left on the Red Trail.

3.6 At the intersection of the Blue Trail, turn right and follow the upper side of the ravine.

4.5 Reach the intersection of the Red/Blue/White Trails and descend to the left. The ravine where many Union soldiers were trapped is on the left. GPS: N33 58.842' / W84 45.699'

5.4 When you reach the visitor center, take time to view the film and exhibits.

GREEN TIP
**If at all possible, camp in established sites.
If there are none, then camp in an unobtrusive area at least
200 feet (70 paces) from the nearest water source.**

15 Red Top Mountain State Park: Homestead and Sweetgum Trails

Nestled along the wooded slopes of a 1,950-acre peninsula surrounded by Allatoona Lake, Red Top Mountain is among Georgia's most popular state parks. Following the damming of the Etowah River by the US Army Corps of Engineers in the 1950s, creating Allatoona Lake, the state set aside land for Red Top Mountain State Park. The Homestead and Sweetgum Trails combine to form a rough "figure eight" network of paths winding through heavily wooded upland forests, creek bottomlands, and along the banks of the lake.

Start: Red Top Mountain headquarters parking area

Distance: 6.2-mile figure eight

Approximate hiking time: 3 to 4 hours

Elevation gain/loss: 179 feet

Trail surface: Compacted soil

Lay of the land: Rolling, wooded slopes, lake inlets, creek bottomlands, upland ridges

Difficulty: Moderate

Seasons: Year-round

Canine compatibility: Leashed dogs permitted

Land status: Georgia State Parks

Fees and permits: Daily parking fee; annual pass available (all units)

Schedule: Open daily from 7 a.m. to 10 p.m.

Nearest town: Cartersville

Maps: USGS Allatoona Dam; maps also available in the visitor center/trading post and headquarters, and on the park website

Trail contact: Red Top Mountain State Park, 50 Lodge Rd., Cartersville 30121; (770) 975-0055; www.gastateparks.org/redtopmountain

Finding the trailhead: Drive north on I-75 to Red Top Mountain Road (exit 285). Turn right (east) and drive 1.8 miles to Marina Road. Turn left (north) and travel 0.7 mile to Lodge Road. Turn right (east) and travel a short distance to the lodge parking area and hike starting point. GPS: N34 09.252' / W84 42.165'

The Hike

This hike begins at the Red Top Mountain headquarters, which is located at the intersection of the trails that form a rough figure eight. Cross the parking area east of the entrance and drive to the sign for the Sweetgum Trail (red blazes). A short distance ahead, the White Tail Nature Trail (white blazes) forks to the right. Continue straight with the red blazes as the Sweetgum Trail parallels the road on a rolling course to an intersection with the Homestead Trail (yellow blazes) at 0.4 mile.

Follow the yellow blazes to the right, descending a short distance where the trail splits to form a loop. Bear right, hiking through a wooded lowland area and along gentle slopes, as the trail first bends left and then to the right. At 0.7 mile the trail reaches a cove on Allatoona Lake and turns left, beginning a steady, moderately

Lake Allatoona cove

strenuous ascent. After a corresponding descent, the trail reaches a viewpoint with a bench at 1.1 miles.

Continue on the trail as it follows a series of switchbacks across slopes above the lake. At 2.1 miles, the path bends left away from the water. A short distance ahead, an unblazed side trail exits from the right, leading to a narrow peninsula. Continue straight, climbing through the upland forest area.

At 2.8 miles, the Homestead Trail bends right and continues ascending along switchbacks, reaching a ridge at 3.0 miles. From that point, the trail turns right and leads gently downward. After a series of turns, the trail closes the northern loop of the Homestead Trail at 3.7 miles. Turn right and ascend a short distance to the entrance road crossing. At this point cross the road and continue the hike, or you may return to the headquarters.

Crossing the road, follow the combined Homestead (yellow blazes) and Sweetgum (red blazes) Trails on a gentle descent to a footbridge at 3.9 miles. A short distance ahead, the two trails diverge. Follow the yellow trail to the right and ascend wooded

Red Top Mountain gets its name from the iron-tinged, reddish clay soils found throughout the area.

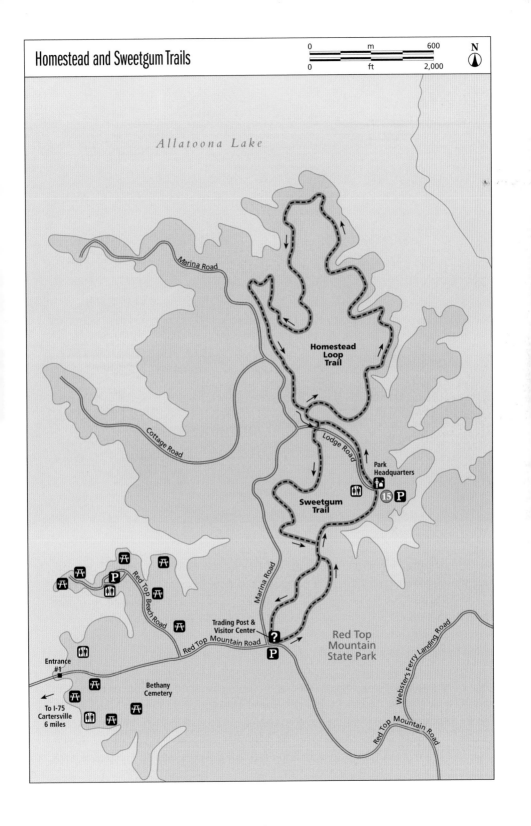

Homestead and Sweetgum Trails

Allatoona Lake

Marina Road

Cottage Road

Homestead Loop Trail

Lodge Road

Park Headquarters

15 P

Sweetgum Trail

Marina Road

Trading Post & Visitor Center

? P

Red Top Mountain Road

Red Top Mountain State Park

Webster's Ferry Landing Road

Red Top Mountain Road

Red Top Beach Road

P

Entrance #1

Bethany Cemetery

To I-75 Cartersville 6 miles

0   m   600
0   ft   2,000

N

Park visitor center and trading post

slopes on a long switchback. After crossing a ridge, the trail bends left and descends to rejoin the Sweetgum Trail. Bear right and continue through a bottomland area.

At 4.4 miles, the trails split again. Follow the yellow blazes and ascend again into the hills above the creek bottom. The trail follows the slope on a rolling track beneath Marina Road, gently descending to the bottomland for a short distance before a short climb to the park's trading post (visitor center) at 5.0 miles.

To return to the headquarters reenter the woods, following the red blazes behind the visitor center parking area, by the tennis courts. Descend to an intersection with the 0.7-mile Visitor Center Loop Trail (green blazes), follow the red blazes to the left, and continue to descend to the creek bottom. The trail follows the lowland area, crossing a small creek on footbridges. At 5.8 miles, reach the merge of the Sweetgum and Homestead Trails and bear right, following the red blazes. The trail follows a gentle ascent along the edge of the lake, passing the intersection with the short 0.7-mile Lakeside Trail (black blazes). At 6.2 miles, exit the trail at the woods by the parking area south of the headquarters.

Miles and Directions

0.0 Begin at the red-blazed Sweetgum Trail sign north of the Red Top Mountain headquarters. GPS: N34 09.252' / W84 42.165'

0.3 Cross the service road.

0.4 Turn right at the intersection with the yellow-blazed Homestead Trail.

0.7 The trail bends to the left above a finger of Allatoona Lake, offering a view of the lake.

1.1 After a steady climb you reach a bench with a lake view. GPS: N34 09.771' / W84 42.129'

2.1 Following rolling switchbacks, the trail ascends away from the lake. GPS: N34 09.994' / W84 42.441'

3.0 The trail bends right after reaching the top of the ascent.

3.7 Turn right and cross the entrance road on the combined Homestead and Sweetgum Trails. GPS: N34 09.455' / W84 42.528'

4.1 As the trails diverge, follow Homestead Trail to the right.

4.6 When the trails rejoin, remain on the Homestead Trail.

5.0 The trading post is also the park visitor center. GPS: N34 08.881' / W84 42.398'

5.8 Follow the combined Homestead and Sweetgum Trails for a short distance, remaining on Sweetgum Trail when paths fork. GPS: N34 09.149' / W84 42.344'

6.2 Exit the woods south of the Red Top Mountain headquarters and the trailhead.

Nearby Attractions

Booth Western Art Museum, 501 Museum Drive, Cartersville 30120; (770) 387–1300; www.boothmuseum.org

Etowah Indian Mounds State Historic Site, 813 Indian Mounds Rd., Cartersville 30120; (770) 387–3747; www.gastateparks.org/etowahindianmounds

NEARBY TRAILS

There are additional short nature trails adjacent to the lodge. The White Tail Trail is 0.5 mile one way; the Visitor Center Loop Trail is a 0.75-mile loop; and the ADA wheelchair-accessible Lakeside Trail is a 0.75-mile loop.

16 Red Top Mountain State Park: Iron Hill Multiuse Trail

This area, in the southern portion of the park, was originally developed as a picnic area with a boating access road. The site has been converted for use as a hiking and mountain-biking trail. The trail gets its name from the nineteenth-century iron mining operations that were carried out in this area. In 1864 Union troops destroyed the mines and blast furnaces used to process the iron ore into metal for the Confederate army. The Cooper Furnace Day Use Area, near Allatoona Dam, preserves a stone blast furnace built in the 1830s.

Start: Gravel parking area off Red Top Mountain Road
Distance: 3.5-mile loop
Approximate hiking time: 2 hours
Elevation gain/loss: 53 feet
Trail surface: Compacted soil and ground gravel
Lay of the land: Rolling forest land, streambeds, and lakeshore areas
Difficulty: Easy due to distance and gentle grades
Seasons: Year-round
Other trail users: Mountain bicyclists

Canine compatibility: Leashed dogs permitted
Land status: Georgia State Parks
Fees and permits: Daily parking fee; annual pass available (all units)
Schedule: Open daily from 7 a.m. to 10 p.m.
Nearest town: Cartersville
Maps: USGS Allatoona Dam; maps also available at the trading post and headquarters, as well as on the park website
Trail contact: Red Top Mountain State Park, 50 Lodge Rd., Cartersville 30121; (770) 975-0055; www.gastateparks.org/redtopmountain

Finding the trailhead: Travel north on I-75 to Red Top Mountain Road (exit 285). Turn right (east) on Red Top Mountain Road, driving past the intersection with Marina Road at 1.8 miles, and continue as the main road bends right past the park's trading post. After passing the campground access road, Webster's Ferry Landing Road will merge from the left. Continue straight; the road to the Iron Hill parking area is ahead on the right. GPS: N34 08.378' / W84 42.038'

The Hike

From the parking area, the gravel access trail descends a short distance to the Iron Hill Multiuse Loop Trail. Hikers may choose to travel in either direction, and this description follows the path on a counterclockwise route. Be alert for mountain bikers, especially on weekends, when the trail may be quite busy.

The wide path follows a gentle descent to a bridge crossing a ravine above a narrow cove of Allatoona Lake. After crossing the bridge, note a large outcrop of pinkish granite on the hillside to the left of the trail. Continue on a fairly level, winding route, keeping the lake to the right. Within a relatively short distance, cross three more

Rock outcrop along Iron Hill Trail

bridges over intermittent streams as the path gently ascends past picnic tables and a campfire circle area, evidence of the area's earlier use.

At 2.0 miles the path reaches a narrow peninsula that marks the end of the outbound leg of the trail loop. The peninsula is an excellent vantage point for panoramic views of Allatoona Lake and the surrounding Appalachian foothills.

Bend sharply left, past a picnic table, and hike eastward. In the distance, to the right, are the wooded highlands and summit of Iron Hill. Soon, the trail bends away from the water and across an old road. Pass remnants of an abandoned comfort station, and continue by following a rolling route through the woods.

At 2.6 miles, the old road you previously crossed merges from the left and for a short distance becomes the route of the trail. Ahead, you reach an intersection with the now-closed boating access road. Follow the directional arrows on the old access road to the right and, almost immediately, turn left from the road to remain on the Iron Hill Trail (if you continue on the old road it will lead to an abandoned parking area and boat ramp).

Iron Hill Multiuse Trail

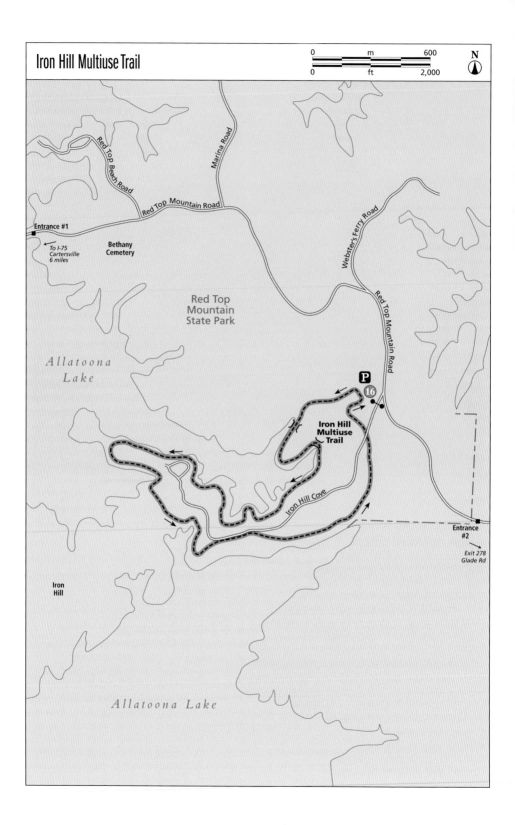

0   m   600

0   ft   2,000

N

Red Top Beech Road

Marina Road

Red Top Mountain Road

Webster's Ferry Road

Red Top Mountain Road

Entrance #1

To I-75
Cartersville
6 miles

Bethany
Cemetery

Red Top
Mountain
State Park

Allatoona
Lake

P

16

Iron Hill
Multiuse
Trail

Iron Hill Cove

Entrance
#2

Exit 278
Glade Rd

Iron
Hill

Allatoona Lake

The trail continues to wind above the lakeshore on a level path. Ahead on the left, pass a heavily eroded hillside showing the deep red, iron-rich soil that drew the miners here more than 150 years ago. At 3.3 miles, the old boating access road crosses the path again. Cross the road and gently descend, following the directional signs as the path reenters the woods on the return to your starting point at 3.5 miles.

Miles and Directions

0.0 The trailhead is at the end of a large gravel parking area. GPS: N34 08.378' / W84 42.038'

0.6 Cross the bridge, following the level walk above the lake. GPS: N34 08.238' / W84 42.142'

0.8 A bridge crosses over a small inlet, which is often dry. GPS: N34 08.117' / W84 42.245'

1.6 To the left of the trail, pass a campfire circle with bleachers. GPS: N34 08.163' / W84 42.568'

2.0 At the end of the outbound leg of the trail, near end of a narrow peninsula, turn left to begin the return. GPS: N34 08.200' / W84 42.841'

2.6 An old road joins from the left; continue straight. GPS: N34 07.955' / W84 42.469'

2.7 Intersect with an old road leading to a closed boat ramp. GPS: N34 07.965' / W84 42.350'

3.3 Cross the old boating access road. GPS: N34 08.239' / W84 42.002'

3.5 Return to the parking area.

Nearby Attractions

Booth Western Art Museum, 501 Museum Drive, Cartersville 30120; (770) 387-1300; www.boothmuseum.org

Etowah Indian Mounds State Historic Site, 813 Indian Mounds Rd., Cartersville 30120; (770) 387-3747; www.gastateparks.org/etowahindianmounds

GREEN TIP
Consider citronella as an effective natural mosquito repellent.

17 Amicalola Falls State Park Trails

The park's name, "Amicalola," is taken from the Cherokee word for "tumbling waters," an apt description for the 729-foot falls (highest east of the Mississippi River) created when the waters of Little Amicalola Creek cascade from high above a wooded valley. The park features miles of trails, scenic views, campgrounds and picnic areas, a mountaintop hotel, and the state's only hike-in lodge (the Len Foote Hike Inn). Amicalola Falls State Park may be best known as a terminal point for hikers traveling the 2,190-mile Appalachian National Scenic Trail (AT), which begins on Springer Mountain north of the park.

Start: Parking area by Amicalola Falls Lodge at the top of the falls
Distance: 4.1-mile circuit of interconnected loops
Approximate hiking time: 3 to 4 hours
Elevation gain/loss: 821 feet
Trail surface: Mix of compacted soil, gravel, ground-up rubber tires, and steps
Lay of the land: Dense woods, steep slopes, creek valley
Difficulty: Strenuous due to steep terrain and many stairs
Season: Year-round
Canine compatibility: Leashed dogs permitted

Land status: Georgia Department of Natural Resources
Fees and permits: Daily fee; annual state parks pass available
Schedule: Open daily from 7 a.m. to 10 p.m.
Nearest town: Dawsonville
Maps: USGS Nimblewell; park maps also available at the visitor center and from the state parks website
Trail contact: Amicalola Falls State Park, 240 Amicalola Falls State Park Rd., Dawsonville 30354; (706) 265-4703; www.amicalolafalls lodge.com

Finding the trailhead: From Atlanta, follow GA 400 north to Highway 53 (just past North Georgia Premium Outlets Mall). Turn left (west) on Highway 53 and drive 6.6 miles to the Dawsonville Square. From the square, continue north on GA 136 for 11.8 miles to GA 183. Follow GA 183 for 1.2 miles, then turn right (east) on GA 52. Travel GA 52 for 1.5 miles and turn left to enter the park. Turn left at the visitor center and climb steeply on the summit road to the Amicalola Falls Lodge parking area. The trail begins north of the lodge. GPS: N34 34.082' / W84 14.758'

The Hike

From the Amicalola Falls Lodge parking area, descend the steps and follow the trail 0.2 mile down to the falls overlook. After glancing down the spine of the falls and to the valley beyond, continue a short distance to the West Ridge staircase, where you will descend 475 steps to the West Ridge Trail. At the bottom of the staircase, you may turn left and walk a short distance to the Upper Falls Overlook for an exceptional view of the falls.

Rubberized trail near Amicalola Falls upper overlook

Amicalola Falls from upper overlook platform

Retrace your steps and follow the West Ridge Trail on a gentle ascent along the slope to the West Ridge Spring parking area at 0.7 mile (this section of the trail is composed of ground-up tires). Cross the parking lot and reenter the woods on the Spring Trail (orange blazes) as it descends along wooded slopes to an intersection with the Mountain Laurel Loop Trail (green blazes).

Turn right on the Mountain Laurel Trail, passing through stands of namesake mountain laurel, and follow a ridge a short distance before descending on switchbacks as the trail turns northward. The Mountain Laurel Trail ends at an intersection with the Creek Trail (yellow blazes) at 1.8 miles. Continue straight on the Creek Trail, following the slope contour before descending to a reflecting pond by the park road.

Ahead, the red-blazed Base of the Falls Trail leads to the Lower and Upper Falls Overlooks. You may climb on steep switchbacks to the lower overlook platform and continue upward by trail and 175 steps to the upper platform at the base of the West Ridge Trail staircase. (The round-trip from the reflecting pond to the upper platform will add 0.6 mile to your hike.) From the reflecting pond, turn south and walk through the picnic area on the Base of the Falls Trail to the park visitor center at 3.2 miles.

Exit the courtyard at the back of the visitor center and pass beneath a stone arch before reentering the woods on the Appalachian Trail Approach Trail (note the AT

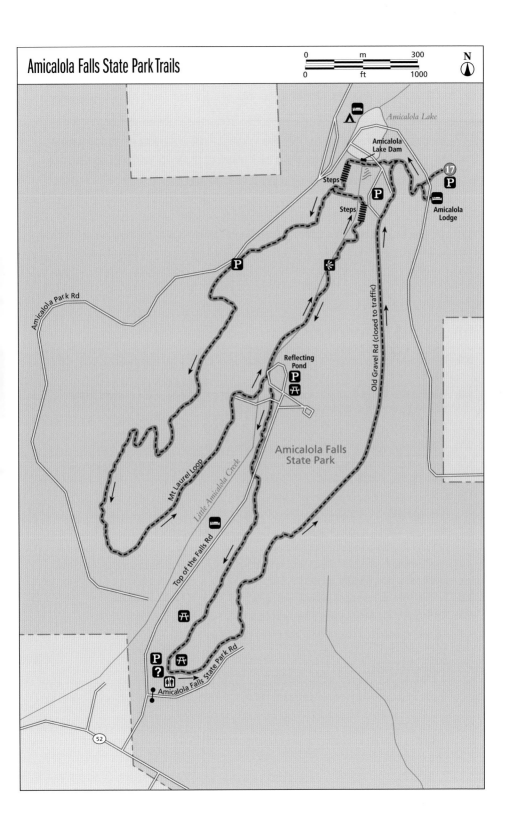

Amicalola Falls State Park Trails

0   m   300
0   ft   1000

N

Amicalola Lake

Amicalola Lake Dam

17

Steps

P

Amicalola Lodge

Steps

Old Gravel Rd (closed to traffic)

P

Amicalola Park Rd

Reflecting Pond

P

Amicalola Falls State Park

Mt Laurel Loop

Little Amicalola Creek

Top of the Falls Rd

P

?

Amicalola Falls State Park Rd

52

historical marker at the visitor center). The path steadily ascends along a series of long switchbacks, passing through mountain laurel thickets and crossing a footbridge, before intersecting with an old service road (closed to automobiles). Turn left and climb, at times steeply, along the road to the Top of the Falls parking area at 4.0 miles. Beyond the parking area, turn right and retrace your steps to the starting point in the lodge parking area at 4.1 miles.

Miles and Directions

0.0 From the Amicalola Lodge parking area, descend the steps to the falls overlook. GPS: N34 34.082' / W84 14.758'

0.2 Take the West Ridge Staircase and descend through switchbacks and 475 steps to the West Ridge Trail. GPS: N34 34.051' / W84 14.661'

0.4 Turn left for the Upper Falls Overlook. GPS: N34 34.006' / W84 14.687'

0.7 At the West Ridge Spring parking area, follow the orange-blazed Spring Trail.

1.1 Turn right at the intersection of the Mountain Laurel Trail and follow the green blazes. GPS: W34 33.728' / W84 14.963'

1.8 Continue straight when you merge with the Creek Trail, following the yellow blazes. GPS: N34 33.693' / W84 15.010'

2.2 When you reach the reflecting pond and Base of Falls Trail, proceed north to the falls overlook platforms (0.6-mile round-trip).

3.2 After walking through the picnic area, stop at the visitor center across from Little Amicalola Creek. GPS: N34 33.466' / W84 14.942'

3.6 Turn left and walk along the gravel road. GPS: N34 33.674' / W84 14.663'

4.0 At the Top of the Falls parking area, bear right. GPS: N34 34.09' / W84 14.618'

4.1 Retrace your steps on the access trail to the starting point.

Nearby Attractions

Dahlonega Gold Museum State Historic Site, #1 Public Square, Dahlonega 30533; (706) 864-2257; www.gastateparks.org/dahlonegagoldmuseum

18 Sweetwater Creek State Conservation Park Trails

This day-use park offers boating and fishing on 215-acre Sparks Reservoir, as well as hikes on trails that meander along Sweetwater Creek and through the surrounding hills. The park opened in 1976 and preserves both the serene beauty of woods and waters and the ghostly ruins of the historic mill operated by the New Manchester Manufacturing Company from 1849 until it was destroyed by Union cavalry on July 9, 1864. The park features more than 8 miles of color-blazed trails that trace paths to the ruins, along Sweetwater Creek, and into the surrounding hills.

Start: Parking area by the visitor center
Distance: 6.5 miles of interconnecting loops
Approximate hiking time: 4 hours
Elevation gain/loss: 389 feet
Trail surface: Compacted soil, exposed rock, sandy floodplain
Lay of the land: Upland forest, slopes and bluffs, river floodplain
Difficulty: Moderate to strenuous
Seasons: Year-round
Canine compatibility: Leashed dogs permitted
Land status: Georgia State Parks and Historic Sites

Fees and permits: Daily parking fee; annual pass available (all units)
Schedule: Open daily from 7 a.m. to 10 p.m.
Nearest town: Austell
Maps: USGS Austell, Mableton, Ben Hill, and Campbellton; maps also available at the visitor center and on the park website
Trail contact: Sweetwater Creek State Conservation Park, 1750 Mount Vernon Rd., Lithia Springs 30122; (770) 732-5871; www.gastateparks.org/sweetwatercreek

Finding the trailhead: Drive west on I-20 to Thornton Road (exit 44). Turn left (south) and cross the bridge over the interstate. In 0.5 mile, turn right (west) on Blair's Bridge Road and follow it for 2.3 miles to Mount Vernon Road. Turn left (south), and drive 1.6 miles to the park entrance on Factory Shoals Road. Turn left (east), and follow the entrance road to the visitor center parking area. GPS: N33 45.224' / W84 37.706'

The Hike

From the parking area adjacent to the visitor center, this hike follows three of the park's blazed trails, the White Trail, the Red (History) Trail, and the Yellow (Sweetwater Creek) Trail.

Begin your hike by descending on the Red Trail a short distance to the intersection with the Yellow Trail. Continue down the Red Trail to the banks of Sweetwater Creek at 0.2 mile. Bear right and follow the old mill road along the creek to an overlook above the first series of shoals. Below the overlook are remains of the original millrace. Continue another 0.5 mile to an observation platform with an

Factory Ruins Trail above Sweetwater Creek shoals

informational sign above the stabilized ruins of the New Manchester Mill. Continue on the Red Trail, descending on wooden steps to the creek bank.

Bear right and follow the trail as it traces a very rocky course above the creek, reaching a small stream with a bridge before steeply ascending to a bluff that provides an excellent view of the shoaled waters. The path descends and continues along the

White Trail climbing above Sweetwater Creek

creek, ascending to a wooden platform overlooking Sweetwater Creek Falls at 1.1 miles. This is the terminal point for the Red Trail. The white-blazed Jack's Hill Trail intersects from the right and extends along the creek bank. Turn right on the White Trail as it bends steeply away from the water on wooden steps and climbs heavily wooded slopes into the upland hills.

Sweetwater Creek

The White Trail follows the contours of the slopes on a rolling path, passing through a lush area of ferns and undergrowth before rejoining the Red Trail at 1.9 miles. Retrace your steps past the mill observation platform and bear left as the White Trail forks away from the creek a second time. The path ascends steadily over broad ridges and shallow stream valleys as it climbs to a terminal point behind the visitor center at 3.2 miles.

To continue the hike, retrace your steps to the Red Trail and descend again to the intersection with the Yellow (Sweetwater Creek) Trail; continue straight to follow the trail as it follows the curving slope on a gentle descent to a footbridge over a small stream where it flows into the creek. Bend left and cross the stream, following the Yellow Trail as it winds along the floodplain.

At 4.2 miles, the path reaches an old road bridge across Sweetwater Creek. Turn right, crossing the bridge, and make another right on the opposite bank, descending on wooden steps to the path. A short distance ahead is the starting point for a loop that climbs, at times very steeply, into the surrounding hills.

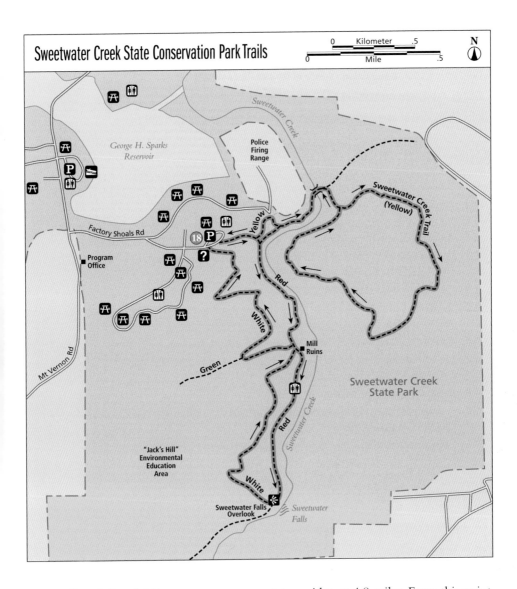

0   Kilometer   .5

0   Mile   .5

N

George H. Sparks
Reservoir

Police
Firing
Range

Sweetwater Creek

Sweetwater Creek Trail
(Yellow)

Factory Shoals Rd

Yellow

18 P

?

Program
Office

Red

White

Green

Mill
Ruins

Sweetwater Creek
State Park

Mt Vernon Rd

Red

Sweetwater Creek

"Jack's Hill"
Environmental
Education
Area

White

Sweetwater Falls
Overlook

Sweetwater
Falls

Bear left and follow a strenuous ascent to a ridge at 4.8 miles. From this point, the path traces an undulating course across several ridges before beginning a steady descent back down toward the creek along a trail marked by several large rock outcrops.

Reach the creek bottom at 5.6 miles and the intersection closing the loop at 6.0 miles. At this point, retrace your steps across the old bridge, along the floodplain, and over the small footbridge to the intersection of the Yellow Trail and an unblazed path along the creek. Follow the unmarked trail a short distance to the Red Trail and ascend back to the starting point in the parking area at 6.5 miles.

PLATINUM DESIGN

The park's visitor center draws crowds of its own. The building has been LEED (Leadership in Energy and Environmental Design) certified by the US Green Building Council at the "platinum" level, one of approximately 300 structures in the world to earn this rating.

Miles and Directions

0.0 Begin at the parking area by the visitor center. GPS: N33 45.224' / W84 37.706'

0.2 Turn right along the old Factory Road.

0.7 The observation deck above the mill ruins offers a good view of the shoals. Turn right at the bottom of the steps and follow the Red Trail. GPS: N33 44.877' / W84 37.410'

1.1 Take the White Trail and ascend on steep wooden steps above the falls. GPS: N33 44.504' / W84 37.509'

1.9 The White Trail forks to the left past the mill ruins.

3.2 The White Trail reaches the visitor center. Retrace your steps on the Red Trail to reach the Yellow Trail.

3.5 Go straight on the Yellow Trail at the intersection with the Red Trail.

4.2 Cross the old road bridge over Sweetwater Creek and turn right on the Yellow Trail. GPS: N33 45.340' / W84 37.346'

4.8 Reach the crest of the ridge above the creek.

6.0 Following completion of the Yellow Trail loop, retrace your steps to the visitor center. GPS: N33 45.303' / W84 37.283'

6.5 Back at the trailhead, enjoy the outstanding visitor center. (See sidebar for details.)

Nearby Attractions

Six Flags over Georgia, 275 Riverside Parkway, Austell 30168; (770) 739-3400; www .sixflags.com/overgeorgia (seasonal)

19 Charlie Elliott Wildlife Center

This 6,400-acre wildlife center, operated by the Georgia Department of Natural Resources, features a network of color-blazed foot trails that wind across old pasture lands, through bottomland hardwoods, beneath upland pine forests, along the shores of man-made ponds and lakes, and around an unusual granite outcrop. An excellent starting point for your trek is the visitor center, with exhibits, a reproduction of Charlie Elliott's writing studio and library, and a wild bird observation room. The center also hosts educational programs throughout the year, with many events held at a nearby conference center and banquet hall.

Start: Trail sign in front of visitor center
Distance: 4.8-mile circuit of interconnected loops
Approximate hiking time: 2 to 3 hours
Elevation gain/loss: 128 feet
Trail surface: Compacted dirt and grass
Lay of the land: Bottomland and upland forests, open meadows
Difficulty: Easy to moderate based on distance and terrain
Seasons: Year-round
Canine compatibility: Leashed dogs permitted

Land status: Georgia Department of Natural Resources
Fees and permits: Free
Schedule: The wildlife center is open 9 a.m. to 4:30 p.m. Mon through Sat
Nearest town: Covington
Maps: USGS Farrar; trail maps also available at visitor center and on the website
Trail contact: Charlie Elliott Wildlife Center, Georgia Department of Natural Resources, Wildlife Resources Division, 543 Elliott Trail, Mansfield 30055; (770) 784-3059; http://georgiawildlife.com/charlieelliott

Finding the trailhead: Drive east on I-20, past Covington, to GA 11 (exit 98). Turn right (south) on GA 11 for 12.0 miles. Turn left (east) on Marben Farm Road, (note Wildlife Center entrance sign), and travel 0.4 mile to Elliott Trail. Turn right (south) and follow the road for 0.3 mile to the visitor center. GPS: N33 27.972' / W83 44.379'

Start your trek at the visitor center with exhibits, a reproduction of Charlie Elliott's writing studio and library, and a wild bird observation room.

The Hike

Beginning at the signed trailhead to the right of the visitor center front entrance, walk about 50 yards to an intersection of the Red (Clubhouse) Trail and Blue (Granite Outcrop) Trail. Turn left and follow the Red Trail behind the visitor center as it descends through a creek bottom and crosses a footbridge before gradually climbing to the other side. At the intersection with the White (Greenhouse Lake) Trail at 0.3 mile, bear left, following the White Trail as it passes an outdoor classroom area and crosses several footbridges over small streams.

Split rail fence on edge of granite outcrop on Blue (Granite Outcrop) Trail

At 0.5 mile, the path enters an open meadow by Pigeonhouse Lake, bending along the eastern side of the lake on a wide, grass path. Continue straight, past a fork of the White Trail, following the northern shore of the small lake as the trail bends east and then south, reaching a clearing with a tree-shaded lakeside shelter at 1.0 mile.

CHARLIE ELLIOTT

The wildlife center is dedicated to Covington, Georgia, native Charlie Elliott (1906–2000), first director of Georgia State Parks (1937–38), commissioner of the Georgia Department of Natural Resources (1938–41), and first director of the Georgia Game and Fish Commission (1943–49). He was also a prolific writer, authoring nineteen books and thousands of articles on outdoor recreation, conservation, hunting, and fishing. In addition, Elliott was southeastern field editor for *Outdoor Life* from 1950–2000, and served as a columnist for the *Atlanta Journal* and *Atlanta Constitution* newspapers for many years.

The Charlie Elliott Chapter of the Atlanta Astronomy Club meets one evening each month to view the night sky far from city lights. The public is welcome to join in the observing. Information on specific dates each month is at www.atlantaastronomy.org.

Lichen-covered boulder on Blue (Granite Outcrop) Trail

Continue along the White Trail as it bends west and reenters the woods beside the lake at 1.2 miles. Turn left at a trail fork beneath a massive oak tree (the straight trail closes the loop and retraces the route to the visitor center).

The path gently descends through second-growth hardwood forest. Follow a streambed to a lowland area and a rock crossing of an intermittent stream before climbing easily to an intersection with the Red Trail at 1.6 miles. Turn left and follow the Red Trail as it traces a course above Clubhouse Lake. The path bends left away from the water, crosses beneath lowland hardwoods and across a creek bottom, then climbs to a level path through a pine forest before reaching an outdoor classroom by a lakeside clearing at 2.1 miles.

Just south of the clearing, pass a comfort station before descending on wooden steps and passing in front of the Brooke Ager Discovery Center (classroom building). Cross an earthen dam separating Clubhouse and Margery Lakes and bend right, ascending back into the woods. At a signed intersection a few yards ahead, turn sharply left on the Yellow (Murder Creek) Trail and follow it on a winding course above Margery Lake. At 2.7 miles, the path bends away from the water and moderately ascends past a large pile of stacked stones above Murder Creek. The path continues to climb to an intersection with the Blue (Granite Outcrop) Trail at 3.5 miles.

Blue-blazed Granite Outcrop Trail

Bend left on the Blue Trail, cross a footbridge over Murder Creek, and ascend on a switchback to a left turn as the path follows the outer edge of a low, exposed outcrop of granite. The trail follows the outer edge of the rock as it bends north, briefly following an old road, then descends again toward the creek bottom, crossing a footbridge at 4.0 miles. The trail follows the creek bottom for a short distance and passes an intersection leading back to the Yellow Trail before climbing over a ridge and descending across the road. Return to the starting point by the visitor center at 4.8 miles.

Charlie Elliott Wildlife Center

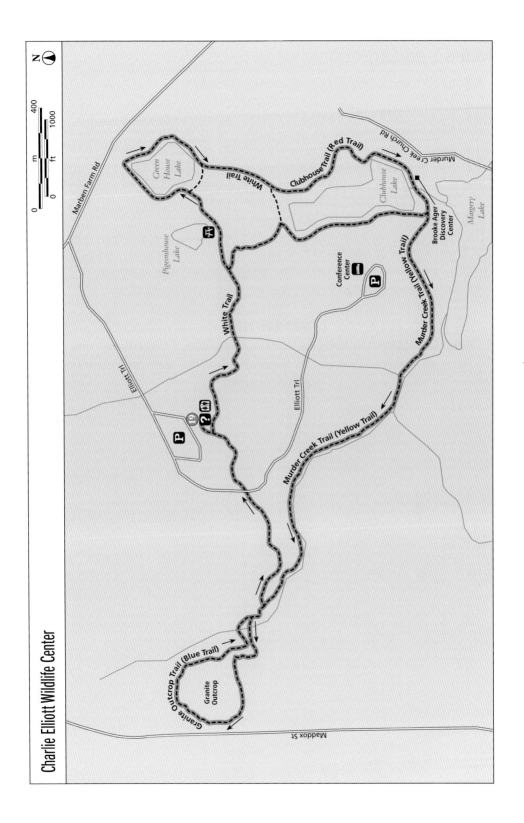

Miles and Directions

0.0 The trail begins to the right of the visitor center entrance. GPS: N33 27.972' / W83 44.379'

0.5 Reach a meadow by Pigeonhouse Lake after crossing several short footbridges. GPS: N33 27.918' / W83 43.869'

1.0 There is a sheltered picnic area by the lake. GPS: N33 28.036' / W83 43.708'

1.6 At the intersection of the Red and White Trails, turn left. GPS: N33 27.762' / W83 43.809'

2.1 In a clearing at the end of a lush pine forest is the Brooke Ager Discovery Center, located beside Clubhouse Lake. GPS: N33 27.547' / W83 43.713'

2.4 After crossing the earthen dam, take a left onto the Yellow Trail.

3.5 Turn left at the intersection with the Blue Trail and cross the footbridge over Murder Creek. GPS: N33 27.728' / W83 44.213'

4.4 Complete the loop around a rock outcrop, turning left to return to the visitor center.

4.8 When you return to the visitor center, take some time to enjoy the many displays.

GREEN TIP

Keep to established trails as much as possible. If there aren't any, stay on surfaces that will be least affected, like rock, gravel, dry grasses, or snow.

Honorable Mentions

D. Allatoona Pass Trails: Old Allatoona Road, Cartersville (Managed by Red Top Mountain State Park) (www.ga stateparks.org/redtopmountain)

Allatoona Pass preserves the October 1864 site of fighting between Union and Confederate troops. The site was a critical point where the Western & Atlantic Railroad crossed the Etowah River, and Confederates attacked in a futile effort to disrupt General Sherman's supply lines. Foot trails (3.4 miles) follow the route of the now-vanished railway beneath a deep cut in the surrounding hills, and wind steeply to a ridge crest where evidence of a Union artillery position is still visible.

The site may be reached by exiting I-75 at Emerson/Allatoona Road (exit 283) and driving east for 0.5 mile. Cross the railroad tracks and bear left to a parking area beneath a levee on Allatoona Lake. The trail begins just north of the parking area.

E. Fort Yargo State Park Trails, 210 South Broad St., Winder 30680; (770) 867-3489; www.gastateparks.org/fortyargo

Surrounding 260-acre Marbury Creek Reservoir, the park features the Will-A-Way Recreation Area, an accessible group camp for developmentally challenged youth and adults, and the wooden blockhouse of Fort Yargo, built in 1792 to protect settlers on the northern frontier. In addition to the group camp, the park offers a campground, picnic areas, and boating facilities. A 12-mile network of hiking trails winds through the piedmont woods and along the shores of the lake.

The park may be reached from Atlanta by traveling north on I-85 to GA 316. Drive east on GA 316 for 21 miles. Turn left (north) toward Winder on GA 81 and drive 3.4 miles. The park entrance will be on the right. Difficulty is easy to moderate based on trail length.

F. Hard Labor Creek State Park Trails, 5 Hard Labor Creek Rd., Rutledge 30663; (706) 557-3001; www.gastateparks.org/hardlaborcreek

This 5,800-acre park draws its name from a stream believed to have been named by slaves who once tilled the fields of antebellum cotton plantations that surrounded it. In the 1930s, Hard Labor Creek State Park was developed from abandoned and eroded lands by the Civilian Conservation Corps (CCC). Enrollees built the park's two lakes, group camps, original trails, and several other historic structures. The popular golf course was laid out in the 1960s. Hard Labor Creek offers 2.5 miles of hiking on two nature trails, and 22 miles of mixed-use trails open to hikers and equestrians. The trails are rated from easy to moderate based on distance and terrain.

The park may be reached from Atlanta by traveling east on I-20 to Newborn Road (exit 105). At the ramp, turn left (north), and drive 3.6 miles to Rutledge. Cross the railroad tracks and turn left (west) onto East Main Street, then right (north) onto Fairplay Road. Travel 2.7 miles and turn left (west) onto Knox Chapel Road. The visitor center is ahead on the right.

G. Panola Mountain State Park Trails, 2620 GA 155 SW, Stockbridge, 30281; (770) 389-7801; www.gastateparks.org/panolamountain

Established to protect the rare plants and fragile environment on and around the bare rock of 100-acre Panola Mountain (an outcrop of exposed granite similar to nearby Arabia and Stone Mountains), the 600-acre day-use park features a 1.0-mile Fitness Trail, a 2.0-mile Forest Trail, and a limited-access 3.5-mile loop trail to the summit of the mountain that is open only during scheduled group hikes or by appointment. The visitor center offers exhibits on the mountain's geology and local natural and human history.

The park may be reached from Atlanta by traveling east on I-20 to Wesley Chapel Road (exit 68). Turn right (south) on Wesley Chapel, drive 0.2 mile to Snapfinger Road (GA 155), and turn left, continuing southeast. Drive 6.0 miles and the park entrance is on the left. The Forest and Fitness Trails are easy; the Panola Mountain Loop Trail is moderately difficult due to distance and terrain.

H. Sweetwater Creek State Park: Jacks Hill Trail, 1750 Mount Vernon Rd., Lithia Springs, GA 30122, (770) 732-5871; www.gastateparks.org/sweetwatercreek

This white-blazed, 3.0-mile trail connects with the Red Trail, offering a longer hike into the more remote parts of the park. The path winds through rugged hills, along the banks of Jack's Branch, and across a meadow that marks the site of the long-vanished Jack's Hill farming community.

You may access the trail from the park's visitor center or at the end of the Red Trail by the Sweetwater Creek rapids. The trail's difficulty is moderate to strenuous due to the terrain. In addition, the Orange Trail adds a 2.3-mile lollipop to the Yellow Trail loop.

GREEN TIP
For rest stops, go off-trail so others won't have to get around you. Head for resilient surfaces without vegetation.

Local Parks
and Gardens

The Atlanta region is blessed with a wide variety of community parks, linear pathways, and private and public gardens that preserve the area's diverse history and natural beauty.

Boardwalk side trail through Heritage Park

20 Piedmont Park Trails

For more than a century, this 238-acre park, 2 miles north of downtown, has served as Atlanta's "common ground," hosting Confederate veterans, US presidents, musicians (from John Philip Sousa to the Allman Brothers), baseball games, and the state's first football game (an 1892 contest between Georgia and Auburn). The park was designed by the Olmsted Brothers for the 1895 Cotton States and International Exposition, which drew more than a million visitors. While Piedmont is a park for recreation and "people-watching," the green space is home to more than 175 species of birds. The nationally renowned Atlanta Botanical Garden occupies the park's northern quarter. Plans are in development for further expansion of the park.

Start: At the parking deck adjacent to the Atlanta Botanical Garden and Welcome Plaza
Distance: 4.6-mile loop with a lollipop to the Northwoods and Piedmont Commons
Approximate hiking time: 3 hours
Elevation gain/loss: 92 feet
Trail surface: Grass, pavement, mulch, and asphalt
Lay of the land: Rolling hills with open meadows and lakes
Difficulty: Easy to moderate
Seasons: Year-round
Other trail users: Inline skaters, bicyclists
Canine compatibility: Leashed dogs permitted; dogs may run free in the gated dog park
Land status: City of Atlanta Department of Parks and Recreation and Piedmont Park Conservancy

Fees and permits: Free
Schedule: Open daily from 6 a.m. to 11 p.m.; guided tours are offered on Saturday at 11 a.m.
Nearest town: Atlanta
Maps: USGS Northeast Atlanta and Northwest Atlanta; maps also available from the visitor center or on the Piedmont Park Conservancy website
Trail contact: Piedmont Park Conservancy, PO Box 7795, Atlanta 30357-0795; (404) 875-7275; www.piedmontpark.org
City of Atlanta Department of Parks and Recreation, 233 Peachtree St., Suites 1600/1700 Atlanta 30303; (404) 546-6788; www.atlantaga.gov
Atlanta Botanical Garden, 1345 Piedmont Ave., Atlanta 30309; (404) 876-5859; www.atlantabg.org

Finding the trailhead: Located 3 miles north of downtown Atlanta, Piedmont Park is about a mile east of I-75/85 at the Fourteenth and Tenth Streets exit (exit 250). Follow Tenth Street east, across Piedmont Avenue, to Monroe Drive at 2.5 miles. Turn left (north) and then left (west) on Worcester Drive to the parking deck (fee) shared with the Atlanta Botanical Garden. There is limited street parking in the surrounding neighborhoods. The park is also easily accessible via a 3- to 4-block walk from either the Tenth Street or Arts Center MARTA (Metropolitan Atlanta Rapid Transit Authority) stations. GPS: N33 47.411' / W84 22.380'

The Hike

From the Welcome Plaza adjacent to the parking deck, turn left (north) past the two Promenade ovals and descend steps to follow the Northwoods Trail. Reach Westminster Drive at 0.5 mile, bear right at the BeltLine Access Trail and continue around Piedmont Commons and across bridges above Clear Creek. Retrace your steps to the Promenade and bear left along the path as it gently descends.

Pass beneath a stone bridge (the intersecting trail leads to the dog park) at 1.3 miles and continue east past the Welcome Plaza and bocce ball courts to Park Drive. Turn left and follow the road a short distance, passing the historic Park Drive bridge and along the shores of Lake Clara Meer. Pause at the bridge and gazebo, adjacent to the park pool and bathhouse. Continue straight a short distance to an iconic overlook of the lake and the midtown Atlanta skyline at 1.9 miles.

Retrace your steps a short distance and cross the road, following the paved path past the youth garden and dog park as it encircles the Meadow that was once the park's golf course. Today it is the finish line for the 65,000 participants in the annual July 4th Peachtree Road Race. At 2.6 miles, exit the Meadow by the small overlook plaza, crossing the road and following it a short distance to a stairway

> Piedmont's Dog Park, where well-behaved canines may run free in a fenced enclosure, is listed among the nation's Top 10 dog parks.

Midtown skyline from Lake Clara Meer

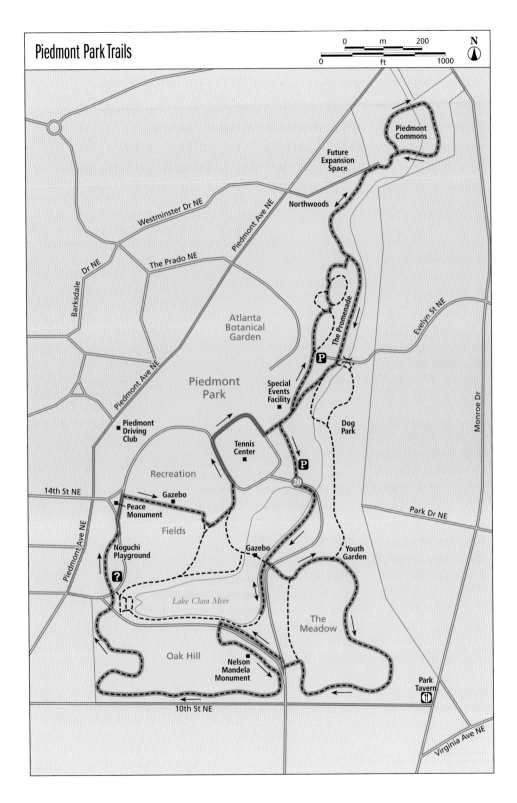

Piedmont Park Trails

0   m   200

0   ft   1000

N

Piedmont Commons

Future Expansion Space

Northwoods

Westminster Dr NE

Piedmont Ave NE

The Prado NE

Barksdale Dr NE

The Promenade

Evelyn St NE

Atlanta Botanical Garden

Monroe Dr

Piedmont Park

Piedmont Ave NE

Special Events Facility

P

Dog Park

Piedmont Driving Club

Tennis Center

Recreation

P

20

Park Dr NE

14th St NE

Gazebo

Peace Monument

Fields

Noguchi Playground

?

Gazebo

Youth Garden

Piedmont Ave NE

Lake Clara Meer

The Meadow

Oak Hill

Nelson Mandela Monument

Park Tavern

10th St NE

Virginia Ave NE

ATLANTA'S FAMOUS FACES

The Cotton States and International Exposition of 1895 brought many of the nation's luminaries to Atlanta. Among them were President Grover Cleveland, who attended the festivities and gave a speech in downtown; composer and renowned band leader John Philip Sousa, who penned the "King Cotton March" for the fair and brought his band to Atlanta to perform it for the first time; and William F. "Buffalo Bill" Cody, who entertained tens of thousands of visitors with his world-famous Wild West Show, which was located in the park's southeastern corner (now the large meadow on Tenth Street).

descending to a lake overlook. Re-cross the road and bend left, then right, as the path ascends the slopes of Oak Hill.

After descending the hill, you will reach the Dockside building at 3.4 miles. Turn left and climb the steps to the Noguchi Playground, with its whimsical playscapes. Continue across the Front Lawn to the old park entrance at 14th Street by the Peace Monument. Turn right (east) and descend steps to the Active Oval, with game fields. On the far side, descend steps on the right and turn left, passing the Mayor's Grove, playground, and Greystone building. Ascend past the tennis center and bear right. Turn left and ascend past the Piedmont Park Conservancy offices to return to the Welcome Plaza at 4.6 miles.

Miles and Directions

0.0 Begin the hike from the Welcome Plaza by the parking deck off Worcester Drive. GPS: N33 47.411' / W84 22.380'

0.5 Reach Westminster Drive and the Piedmont Commons area

1.9 At the Lake Clara Meer Bridge, go to the gazebo and nearby overlook. Then retrace your steps to the trail along the lakeside. GPS: N33 47.128' / W84 22.364'

2.6 Reach the Meadow overlook plaza.

3.4 After descending Oak Hill, reach the Dockside building at the 12th Street access path. GPS: N33 47.001' / W84 22.628'

3.6 The Peace Monument marks the formal park entrance at Fourteenth Street. Descend the steps to cross the Active Oval.

3.9 Pass the Mayor's Grove and Greystone building and ascend past the tennis center. GPS: N33 47.146' / W84 22.454'

4.6 Return to the Welcome Plaza.

Nearby Attractions

High Museum of Art, 1280 Peachtree St., Atlanta 30309; (404) 733-4400; www.high .org

21 BeltLine: Eastside Trail

Utilizing abandoned railroad corridors, the BeltLine is the most comprehensive transportation and economic development project in modern Atlanta's history. It will eventually connect more than forty-five neighborhoods through a network of more than 33 miles of multiuse trails encircling the city. The 3-mile Eastside Trail was the first section completed and links Piedmont Park with the Ponce City Market, passes through the Old Fourth Ward and the Freedom Parkway Trail to the Jimmy Carter Presidential Library, and continues beyond toward the historic Cabbagetown and Reynoldstown neighborhoods.

Start: 10th Street at Monroe Drive, across from Piedmont Park
Distance: 3 miles point-to-point
Approximate hiking time: 1.5 hours one way
Elevation gain/loss: 144 feet
Trail surface: Pavement
Lay of the land: Level to gently rolling along abandoned railroad bed
Difficulty: Easy
Seasons: Year-round
Other trail users: Inline skaters, bicyclists
Canine compatibility: Leashed dogs permitted
Land status: City of Atlanta Department of Parks and Recreation and Atlanta BeltLine Partnership

Fees and permits: Free
Schedule: Open daily from 6 a.m. to 11 p.m.
Nearest town: Atlanta
Maps: USGS Northeast Atlanta and Northwest Atlanta; maps also available from the Atlanta BeltLine website; www.beltline.org
Trail contact: Atlanta BeltLine Partnership, 112 Krog St., Suite 14, Atlanta, GA 30307; (404) 446-4404; www.beltline.org
City of Atlanta Department of Parks and Recreation, 233 Peachtree St., Suites 1600/1700, Atlanta 30303; (404) 546-6788; www.atlantaga.gov

Finding the trailhead: Located 3 miles north of downtown Atlanta, the northern terminus of the Eastside Trail is about 1.3 miles east of I-75/85 at the Tenth Street exit (exit 250). Follow Tenth Street east, across Piedmont Avenue, to Monroe Drive at 2.5 miles. The trailhead is directly ahead. Parking (fee) is available at Park Tavern. There is also parking on neighborhood streets along the BeltLine route, at Ponce City Market, and at Old Fourth Ward Park. A large parking deck on Worcester Drive that serves Piedmont Park and the Atlanta Botanical Garden also provides access to the Eastside Trail via the Montgomery Ferry access path. GPS: N33 46.905' / W84 22.118'

The Hike

From the northern terminus on Monroe Drive across from Piedmont Park, the Eastside Trail climbs a short slope and bends right to follow the old railroad corridor southward. Along the route are numerous displays of public art and sculpture, as well as scenic views of the Atlanta skyline.

Skyline from BeltLine Eastside Trail

At 0.7 mile, adjacent to the sprawling Ponce City Market, cross the old railroad bridge across Ponce de Leon Avenue. The massive building, built by Sears Roebuck and Co. in 1926, has been transformed into a popular destination filled with apartments, shops, cafes, and a rooftop skyline park with special event space and panoramic views of the city.

Continue south to the short Gateway Trail that connects to Old Fourth Ward Park at 1.2 miles. This 17-acre recreational space features ponds and a seasonal splash pad, meandering paths, an amphitheater, picnic areas, a popular skate park, and restrooms. A short distance ahead, after passing beneath Freedom Parkway, you reach the intersection with the PATH trail linking the BeltLine with the Martin Luther King Jr. National Historic District to the west and the Jimmy Carter Presidential Library and historic Inman Park to the east.

The Eastside Trail winds among several trendy eateries and eclectic shops as it continues south, reaching a temporary (through 2018) detour at Edgewood Avenue at 2.4 miles. Follow signs and stairs along Edgewood to Krog Street and turn right,

Public art along the BeltLine Eastside Trail

passing beneath DeKalb Avenue in the artfully decorated Krog Street tunnel. Exit the tunnel, turn left on Wylie Street, and walk a short distance to a right-hand turn on the Eastside Trail extension to the current southern terminal point at Kirkwood Avenue at 3.0 miles. Work continues on the trail, with Phase II construction reaching Memorial Drive in 2019.

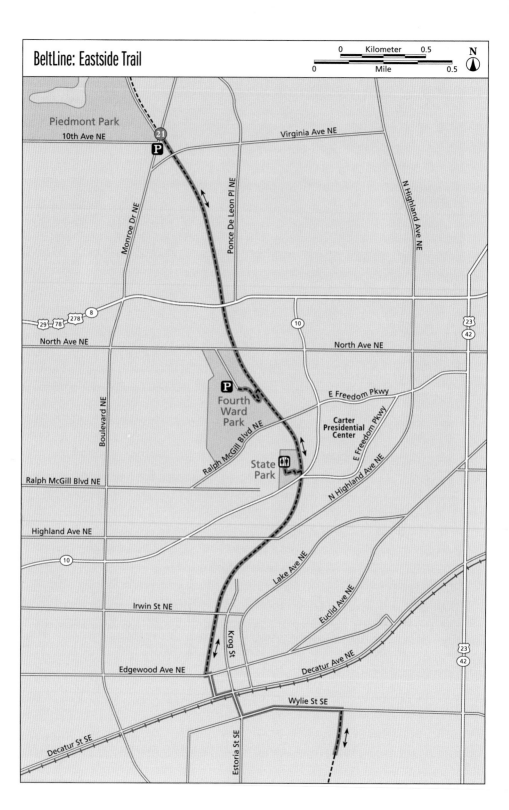

0   Kilometer   0.5

0   Mile   0.5

N

Piedmont Park

10th Ave NE

Virginia Ave NE

21

P

Monroe Dr NE

Ponce De Leon Pl NE

N Highland Ave NE

29 78 278 8

10

23
42

North Ave NE

North Ave NE

P

Fourth
Ward
Park

E Freedom Pkwy

Boulevard NE

Ralph McGill Blvd NE

Carter
Presidential
Center

E Freedom Pkwy

Ralph McGill Blvd NE

State
Park

N Highland Ave NE

Highland Ave NE

10

Lake Ave NE

Euclid Ave NE

23
42

Irwin St NE

Krog St

Edgewood Ave NE

Decatur Ave NE

Wylie St SE

Decatur St SE

Estoria St SE

Miles and Directions

0.0 Start at the northern terminal point of Eastside Trail. GPS: N33 46.905' / W84 22.118'

0.7 Reach the old railroad bridge and access to Ponce City Market. GPS: N33 46.404' / W84 21.845'

1.4 Arrive at the intersection with PATH Freedom Parkway Trail.

2.4 Follow directions at Edgewood Avenue detour. GPS: N33 45.269' / W84 21.907'

2.6 Exit the Krog Street tunnel and turn onto Wylie Street.

3.0 Reach the end of the Eastside Trail at Kirkwood Avenue. GPS: N33 45.012' / W84 21.409'

GREEN TIP

Be green and stylish too—wear clothing made of organic cotton or recycled products.

22 Silver Comet Trail: Mavell Road to Floyd Road

Following the route of the "Silver Comet" train that carried passengers and mail between New York City, Atlanta, and Birmingham from 1947 until 1969, this rail-trail stretches from Smyrna to Alabama, where it joins the Chief Ladiga Trail rising east from Anniston, Alabama. The easternmost section of the trail, this 4.2-mile path links Mavell Road with Floyd Road. Sites along the way include a steel-framed bridge over the East-West Connector; Heritage Park, with side trails leading to ruins of the Concord Woolen Mill, historic Concord Covered Bridge, and a nature center pavilion; and the old railroad tunnel beneath Hurt Road.

Start: Mavell Road parking area
Distance: 4.2 miles point to point
Approximate hiking time: 2 hours
Elevation gain/loss: 152 feet
Trail surface: Asphalt, concrete; compacted soil and wooden boardwalk on side trails
Lay of the land: Rolling, gentle grades
Difficulty: Easy due to distance and level, rolling grade
Seasons: Year-round
Other trail users: Runners, bicyclists, and inline skaters
Canine compatibility: Leashed dogs permitted

Land status: Partnership of Georgia Department of Transportation, Georgia State Parks, Cobb, Paulding, and Polk Counties
Fees and permits: Free
Schedule: Open daily during daylight hours
Nearest town: Mableton
Maps: USGS Mableton; maps also available from the Silver Comet and PATH Foundation websites
Trail contact: PATH Foundation, PO Box 14327, Atlanta 30324; (404) 875-3242; www.pathfoundation.org and www.silvercometga.com

Finding the trailhead: Travel north to I-285 to South Cobb Drive (exit 15). Drive north on South Cobb Drive (exit 15) 1.8 miles to Cooper Lake Road. Turn left (west) and travel 0.7 mile to Mavell Road. Turn left (south) and drive past Nickajack Elementary School. The road ends at the Silver Comet Trail parking area. An access trail leads 1.0 mile east to additional parking at the Highland Station shopping center. This also links to the growing Cumberland Connector Trail System. GPS: N33 50.503' / W84 31.037'

To reach the Floyd Road parking area from I-285, follow South Cobb Drive north for 0.4 mile to the East-West Connector (GA 3). Turn right (west) and drive 5.8 miles to Floyd Road. Turn left (south) and travel 0.7 mile. A parking area by the closed Silver Comet Cycles shop is on the right. GPS: N33 50.820' / W84 35. 122'

The Hike

From the Mavell Road parking area with its depot-style comfort station, follow the trail as it gently descends to the west through a wooded area. Cross a bridge over

Bikers and walkers approach East-West Connector Bridge

Cooper Lake Road at 0.7 mile. From there, the trail follows a rolling, mostly level course to a railroad-style trestle bridge crossing over the East–West Connector at 2.3 miles.

A short distance past the bridge a pedestrian-only side trail to the left descends through Heritage Park to the stabilized ruins of the nineteenth-century Concord Mill. From the ruins, a path to the right leads 0.5 mile to the 140-year-old Concord Covered Bridge, built in 1872 to replace the original structure burned by Union troops during fighting at nearby Ruff's Mill in 1864.

RAILWAY TRAILS

In 1998 the PATH Foundation, in partnership with the Georgia Department of Transportation (GDOT), Georgia State Parks, and the three counties through which the line extended (Cobb, Paulding, and Polk) began planning the multiuse trail along the abandoned railway line.

Silver Comet Trail: Mavell Road to Floyd Road

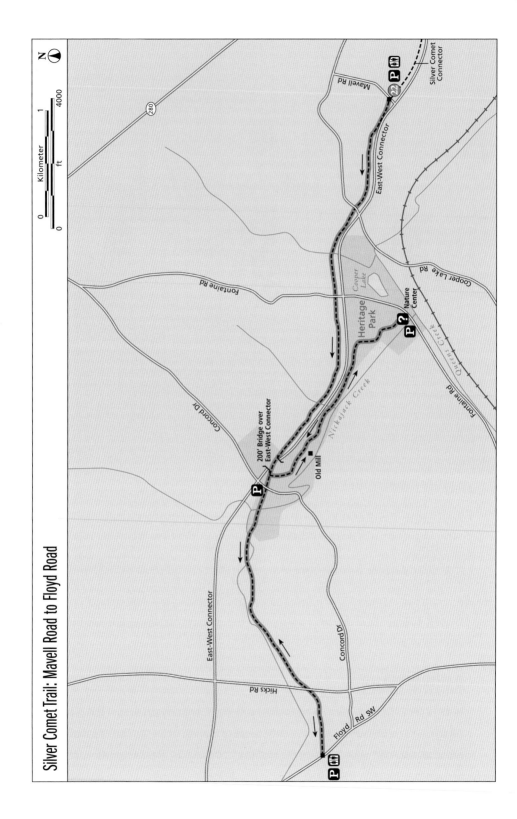

Ruins of old Concord Mill in Heritage Park a short distance from Silver Comet Trail

From that point, retrace your steps back to Concord Mill and continue straight at the intersection to the Silver Comet access trail. The path meanders along the banks of Nickajack Creek before turning sharply right and following a wetlands boardwalk to

The Concord Covered Bridge over Nickajack Creek, located at the western end of the Heritage Park Trail, was constructed in 1872 to replace the bridge burned by Federal troops in 1864. It is the only covered bridge in the Atlanta area still in its original location.

a nature center pavilion and satellite parking area at Fontaine and Nickajack Roads. A round-trip to see all the Heritage Park attractions will add 4 miles to your trek.

Returning to the Silver Comet Trail continue west, past an access trail to Concord Road and through the old railroad tunnel beneath Hurt Road at 3.0 miles. Ahead, you cross Hicks Road (note that Silver Comet Trail travelers may use pole-mounted traffic control buttons at road intersections). At 4.2 miles, reach Floyd Road. Cross over to the parking area by the now closed Silver Comet Cycles to complete your hike of this section.

Miles and Directions

0.0 Begin the Silver Comet Trail at the Mavell Road parking area. GPS: N33 50.503' / W84 31.037'

2.3 Reach the bridge crossing over the East-West Connector. GPS: N33 51.035' / W84 33.339'

3.0 Reach the tunnel that runs beneath Hurt Road.

4.2 Arrive at the end of the route. The closed Silver Comet Cycles store is adjacent to the Floyd Road parking area. GPS: N33 50.822' / W84 35.140'

GREEN TIP
When hiking in a group, walk single file on established trails to avoid widening them. If you come upon a sensitive area, spread out so you don't cut one path through the landscape. Avoid creating new trails where there were none before.

23 Silver Comet Trail: Floyd Road to Florence Road

This path is the Silver Comet Trail's continuation west from Floyd Road. Along this section's 7.3-mile route (one way), the trail passes through a railroad cut, over a trestle bridge with a panoramic view of the Dogwood Country Club, and past a parking area and 1.6-mile side trail leading to Wild Horse Creek Park. Farther west the path skirts the edge of historic Powder Springs (an access trail leads to restaurants and shops). Just beyond town, a boardwalk leads to Lucille Creek Trail; the path climbs across a bridge over the creek and descends to the end point at the Florence Road parking area.

Start: Floyd Road parking area at Silver Comet Depot store
Distance: 7.3 miles point to point
Approximate hiking time: 3 hours
Elevation gain/loss: 147 feet
Trail surface: Asphalt and concrete
Lay of the land: Rolling, gentle grades
Difficulty: Easy to moderate due to distance and level, rolling grade
Seasons: Year-round
Other trail users: Runners, bicyclists, and inline skaters

Canine compatibility: Leashed dogs permitted
Land status: Partnership of Georgia Department of Transportation, Georgia State Parks, Cobb, Paulding, and Polk Counties
Fees and permits: Free
Schedule: Open daily during daylight hours
Nearest towns: Mableton and Powder Springs
Maps: USGS Mableton and Austell; maps also available from the PATH Foundation website
Trail contact: PATH Foundation, PO Box 14327, Atlanta 30324; (404) 875-3242; www.path foundation.org and www.silvercometga.com

---

Finding the trailhead: To reach the Floyd Road parking area, travel on the Atlanta perimeter road, I-285, to South Cobb Drive (exit 15). Turn north for 0.4 mile to the East-West Connector and turn left (west). Drive west 5.8 miles to Floyd Road. Turn left (south) and travel 0.7 mile. The Silver Comet Depot parking area is on the right. GPS: N33 50.822' / W84 35.140'

To reach the Florence Road parking area, continue west on the East-West Connector from the Floyd Road intersection for 2.8 miles to Powder Springs Road. Turn left (west), and follow Powder Springs Road for 2.3 miles to Richard Sailors Parkway, turning right (west). Follow Sailors Parkway for 2.0 miles to Florence Road. The parking area, with a depot-style comfort station, is on the right. GPS: N33 52.173' / W84 42.078'

The Hike

From the Floyd Road parking area, the trail follows a wooded path west. Cross the intersection with Brookwood Road before passing through a deep, heavily shaded railroad cut at 1.3 miles. (*Note:* Trail markers reflect mileage from the zero milepost at the Mavell Road parking area.) At 2.3 miles, the trail crosses over a trestle bridge high

Lucille Creek Side Trail from Silver Comet Trail

above Olley Creek, featuring panoramic views to the left of the Dogwood Country Club golf course.

The path crosses three road intersections (note the pole-mounted traffic control buttons) before reaching a parking area for the Wild Horse Creek Park Access Trail at 4.4 miles. A side trail leads to the Powder Springs city park, which features recreation fields, picnic areas, a BMX biking track, equestrian facilities, and the Ron Anderson Recreation Center with gymnasium and community center. A round-trip hike to Wild Horse Creek Park is 3.2 miles.

Continue west on the Silver Comet Trail, crossing Carter Road, to the small, historic community of Powder Springs, settled in 1839 on former Cherokee lands. At 5.0 miles, a side trail to the left leads to the downtown area featuring restaurants and shops. At 5.9 miles, descend to a busy crossing of Old Lost Mountain Road before climbing to the west on a moderate slope.

Silver Comet Trail: Floyd Road to Florence Road

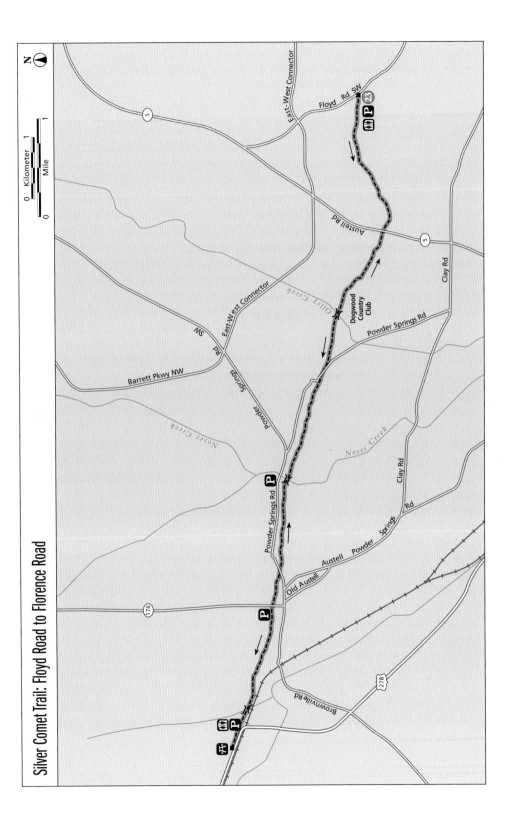

The trail returns to a gentle, rolling course for another mile before reaching an intersection with a switchback trail and boardwalk leading down to Lucille Creek and a wetlands area. From there, the Silver Comet Trail crosses the creek on a high bridge before descending to the Florence Road terminal point at 7.3 miles.

Miles and Directions

0.0 Begin at the Silver Comet Cycles store (closed) adjacent to the Floyd Road parking area. GPS: N33 50.822' / W84 35.140'

2.3 The bridge crosses Olley Creek and the golf course. GPS: N33 51.117' / W84 37.322'

4.4 The access trail to the right goes to the Wild Horse Creek Park. GPS: N33 51.419' / W84 39.395'

5.0 The access trail to the left goes to downtown Powder Springs.

7.3 Arrive at end point. The Florence Road parking area also has trailer parking. GPS: N33 52.173' / W84 42.078'

GREEN TIP

Be courteous of others. Many people visit natural areas for quiet, peace, and solitude, so avoid making loud noises and intruding on others' privacy.

24 Pine Mountain Recreation Area Trails

Following the heavily wooded slopes of 1,562-foot Pine Mountain, north of Red Top Mountain State Park and Allatoona Lake, this recreation area is a Cartersville city park. The park's East Loop Trail is open to hikers every day and to mountain bikers on Wednesday and Saturday. The West Loop Trail is for hikers only. The park is a short distance from the Allatoona Dam visitor center and Cooper's Furnace day-use area, which is accessible by a connecting trail.

Start: Recreation area parking lot off Highway 20 Spur.
Distance: 4.8 miles of connecting loops
Approximate hiking time: 3 to 4 hours
Elevation gain/loss: 691 feet
Trail surface: Compacted soil
Lay of the land: Heavily wooded slopes and ravines; the trail crosses permanent and intermittent streams. The grade of the East Loop is the steeper of the two trails.
Difficulty: Moderate to difficult
Seasons: Year-round
Other trail users: Mountain bicyclists
Canine compatibility: Leashed dogs permitted

Land status: City of Cartersville Parks and Recreation
Fees and permits: Free
Schedule: Trails open during daylight hours
Nearest town: Cartersville
Maps: USGS Allatoona Dam and Cartersville; maps also available from the park website and from the Cartersville Bartow County Convention and Visitor Bureau website, www.visit carolinega.org
Trail contact: Cartersville Parks and Recreation Department, PO Box 1390 / 100 Pine Grove Rd., Cartersville 30120; (770) 387-5626; www.cityofcartersville.org

Finding the trailhead: From Atlanta drive north on I-75 to GA 20 (exit 290), and turn right (north). Turn right (east), again, on GA 20 Spur and follow the road 4.0 miles. After passing Bartow Beach Road on the left, look for the Pine Mountain Recreation Area's gravel parking lot on the right (west). There is also a satellite parking area off I-75 at exit 288. Bear right (east) on Main Street and turn right (south) at signs for Pine Mountain Trail and Komatsu. A parking area will be on the left. There also is parking on Main Street at Komatsu Drive. Extending the hike to historic Cooper Furnace day-use area and back will add about 2.6 miles to your distance. GPS: N34 10.602' / W84 44.224'

The Hike

The hike begins from the eastern trailhead on the GA 20 Spur. From the gravel parking area, the trail quickly ascends past an information sign, bending sharply right and following the slope above.

At 0.1 mile, the trail forks at a terminal point noting the beginning of the East Loop Trail (green blazes). Follow the path to the right and gradually descend. The trail reaches a footbridge across an intermittent stream and bears left on a moderate ascent across a ridge before descending again through lush thickets of mountain laurel to a

Pine Mountain summit

stream-cut ravine called "Whiskey Point" (possibly the site of an old moonshine still). The trail continues to descend between a steep rock outcrop on the left and a small stream on the right.

At 0.6 mile, cross two footbridges and begin a steady climb, on long switchbacks, as the trail ascends the slope of Pine Mountain. After nearly a mile of steady climbing, the path reaches a point beneath the summit at the intersection with the East Pass Trail (blue blazes), which leads to the brown-blazed Summit Trail and beyond to the West Pass Trail (red blaze). Follow the blue blazes to the right, past a cell phone tower as the trail ascends.

At 1.6 miles, the Summit Trail continues straight, while the red-blazed West Pass Trail bends right and begins a descent to the western slopes of the mountain. Follow the Summit Trail 0.1 mile, past rock outcrops, to the top of Pine Mountain. A panoramic view includes Cartersville to the west, and Allatoona Lake and Red Top Mountain State Park to the south. Retrace your steps to the West Pass Trail and turn left, descending a short distance to the intersection with the West Loop Trail (purple blazes).

Following the West Loop trail to the right is a steeper descent but a more moderately difficult return to West Pass Trail. The path follows a series of switchbacks through an area of pine forests and low shrubs and lush groundcover. At 2.3 miles, the

Bridge near Whiskey Point on East Loop Trail

A MONUMENT TO FRIENDSHIP

At the base of Pine Mountain are the ruins of a cold-blast furnace that was once part of the Cooper Iron Works, constructed in the 1830s when the mineral-rich area around Pine and Red Top Mountains was a center of iron mining. The works were purchased by Mark A. Cooper and a business partner in the mid-1840s. To connect their company with the newly completed Western & Atlantic Railroad line in Cartersville, the men borrowed funds to construct the short-line Etowah Railroad. In 1847 Cooper's partner could not pay off his share of the loan, and Cooper purchased his interest in the iron works and railroad. A decade later, Cooper was $100,000 in debt and saw his company sold at auction. Remarkably, Cooper sought help from friends, who loaned him $200,000 to buy back the company. In 1860 he repaid the loan and erected the unique Friendship Monument, which holds the names of the thirty-eight friends who had helped him. Today, the monument stands in Friendship Plaza in downtown Cartersville. During the Civil War, the Etowah Railroad's small engine, *Yonah*, was briefly used by Captain William Fuller's Rebel pursuers during the famous 1862 "Great Locomotive Chase."

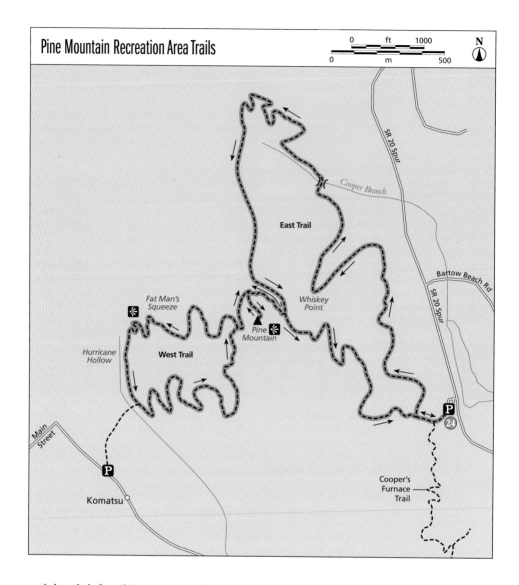

path bends left and intersects with a service road, following the road a short distance before bending right and continuing to descend. A short distance ahead, the trail reaches a prominent outcrop of exposed boulders and a steep switchback called "Fat Man's Squeeze." Beyond, the trail offers views of a fairly deep ravine called "Hurricane Hollow."

The path descends to an area just above the hollow as it bends left and follows a fairly level course. At 2.8 miles, a trail marker denotes the beginning point for the West Loop Trail. The green-blazed path to the right of the main trail leads to a satellite parking area. From this point, the trail crosses a footbridge and begins a long, steady ascent on switchbacks as it climbs the western slope of Pine Mountain. At 3.6

miles, reach the intersection with the West Pass Trail (red blazes) and retrace your steps across the saddle beneath the summit to the blue-blazed East Pass Trail before rejoining the East Loop Trail (green blazes). Bear right and begin a steady descent along switchbacks, reaching the terminal point of the East Loop Trail at 4.7 miles. Follow the access trail a short distance back to the starting point.

Miles and Directions

0.0 The trail ascends to the left of the park information sign. GPS: N34 10.602' / W84 44.224'

0.1 After ascending a switchback to the right, intersect with the terminal point for the East Loop Trail (green blazes). Follow this green-blazed trail to the right for a more gradual ascent of Pine Mountain.

0.6 This area, called "Whiskey Point," has a trail marker noting the elevation of 928 feet.

1.6 Bear right on the blue-blazed East Pass Trail to the brown-blazed Summit Trail and the red-blazed West Pass Trail. GPS: N34 10.747' / W84 44.711'

1.7 Enjoy the view at the summit of Pine Mountain. GPS: N34 10.607' / W84 44.696', elevation 1,562 feet

2.1 Bear right at the intersection with the purple-blazed West Trail.

2.5 The trail reaches prominent rock outcrops at an area called "Fat Man's Squeeze."

2.8 Bear left at the intersection onto the purple-blazed West Loop Trail and begin a gradual ascent. GPS: N34 10.453' / W84 45.091'

3.6 Complete the West Loop Trail and follow the West Pass Trail to the East Pass Trail. GPS: N34 10.566' / W84 45.868'

3.9 Turn right at the East Loop Trail intersection, descending on switchbacks through heavily wooded slopes.

4.8 At the completion of the East Loop Trail, you return to the gravel parking area.

Nearby Attractions

Allatoona Dam Visitor Center, 1138 GA 20 Spur, Cartersville 30121; (678) 721-6700; www.sam.usace.army.mil/Missions/Civil-Works/Recreation/Allatoona-Lake

Tellus Northwest Georgia Science Museum, 100 Tellus Dr., Cartersville 30120; (770) 606-5700; www.tellusmuseum.org

Booth Western Art Museum, 501 Museum Dr., Cartersville 30120; (770) 387-1300; www.boothmuseum.org

Etowah Indian Mounds State Historic Site, 813 Indian Mounds Rd., Cartersville 30120; (770) 387-3747; www.gastateparks.org

25 Pine Log Creek Trails

Nestled in rugged Appalachian foothills, this 275-acre Bartow County recreation area features more than 4 miles of hiking trails across floodplains, through second-growth forests, and over ridges offering vistas of meadows, farm fields, and the slopes of Pine Log Mountain to the south. The trails overlook a pastoral valley that was once home to the Cherokee village of Pine Log before the native people's removal west on the Trail of Tears in the 1830s.

Start: Gravel parking area off GA 140
Distance: 4.7 miles on interconnecting loops
Approximate hiking time: 3 hours
Elevation gain/loss: 507 feet
Trail surface: Compacted soil
Lay of the land: Creek valleys and heavily wooded slopes with several stream crossings on footbridges
Difficulty: Moderate to difficult
Seasons: Year-round
Canine compatibility: Leashed dogs permitted

Land status: Bartow County Parks and Recreation Department
Fees and permits: Free
Nearest town: Waleska
Maps: USGS White East; trail map also posted at trailhead
Trail contact: Bartow County Parks and Recreation Department, 31 Beavers Dr., Cartersville 30120; (770) 387-5149; www.bartowga.org/departments/parksandrecreation/index.php/pine-log-creek-walking-trail.html

Finding the trailhead: From Atlanta travel north on I-75 to US 411 (exit 293) and turn right (north). Drive 8 miles to GA 140 and turn right (east). Travel approximately 3 miles to the park entrance on the left (north) side of the road. The trail begins north of a graveled parking area a short distance off the highway. GPS: N34 20.907' / W84 39.863'

The Hike

From the parking area, the path enters the woods to the north and follows a rolling course marked by pines and young hardwoods before crossing Pine Log Creek on an elevated footbridge at 0.2 mile. After ascending from the floodplain, reach a second bridge at 0.4 mile. Cross and bear right before bending left and following the slope of a low hill to the West Loop Trail at 0.5 mile.

Turn right and cross another bridge before making a sharp left and climbing the slope along several switchbacks to a high point on the trail just beneath the ridge crest. At 0.6 mile, descend to cross a narrow creek valley, then continue past large rocks to Pine Log Creek at 0.9 mile. The path follows the creek a short distance before bending sharply left and ascending away from the water at 1.0 mile.

After a long climb followed by a descent, the trail crosses a bridge and turns right to follow the south-facing slope of a hill. At 1.3 miles, the access path to the East Loop Trail exits to the right. After crossing a footbridge, ascend along a fern-filled creek bed to an intersection. Bear right onto the East Loop and climb more steeply

Pine Log Creek from East Loop Trail

on switchbacks as you meander through stands of mountain laurel to a ridge at 1.6 miles. Follow the ridge through thick pine stands, where openings among the trees offer panoramic views of Pine Log Mountain to the southwest.

Descend across a creek valley and continue along the northern slope of a hillside. At 2.0 miles, you reach a crossing of an intermittent streambed. Turn right and climb the south-facing slope, reaching a ridge crest at 2.2 miles with exceptional winter views of mountains and meadows. Follow a boulder-strewn slope above a small glade and reach the Quarry Pond Trail intersection at 2.3 miles. Take the short path to the right to see the pond created when men of the Depression-era Civilian Conservation Corps (CCC) quarried stone from these hills for erosion control projects.

Retrace your steps to the East Loop Trail and turn right to begin a gradual climb on switchbacks as the path bends westward. Follow the path past an old deer-hunting stand and across an intermittent stream to close the loop at 3.0 miles. Continue to the intersection with the West Loop Trail. For a short return to the parking area, turn left.

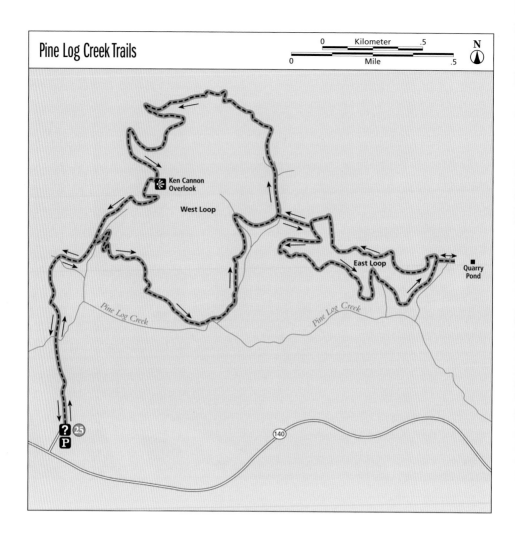

Pine Log Creek Trails

Kilometer

Mile

N

Ken Cannon Overlook

West Loop

East Loop

Quarry Pond

Pine Log Creek

Pine Log Creek

140

25

If you wish to continue on the West Loop Trail, turn right and begin a steady ascent, crossing a footbridge and following a gentle slope. At 3.2 miles, the trail ascends more steeply as it follows the west-facing slopes. After traversing two long switchbacks, the trail traces a zigzag course on short switchbacks as it nears the high ridges. Soon, the route bends sharply left, reaching the trail's high point near a summit marked by shortleaf pines at 3.7 miles.

After a short distance, the trail begins a gradual, then steeper, descent of the southwest-facing slopes along a series of long switchbacks. At 3.9 miles, the trail reaches the Ken Cannon Overlook, an opening in the trees with a panoramic view of Pine Log Mountain to the south, and farm fields and meadows to the west. The path continues descending to a creek valley lush with mountain laurel and ferns. Near

Climbing on the West Loop Trail ▶

the base of the valley, the path levels, following the creek to the starting point for the West Trail Loop at 4.3 miles.

From this point, continue straight to retrace your steps to the parking area at 4.7 miles.

Miles and Directions

0.0 Start from the gravel parking area off GA 140. GPS: N34 20.907' / W84 39.863'

0.5 Turn right at the intersection of the access trail and the West Loop Trail and cross the bridge. GPS: N34 21.243' / W84 39.820'

0.9 Descend to Pine Log Creek and take a right. GPS: N34 21.123' / W84 39.524'

1.3 Turn right and cross the footbridge to follow the East Loop Trail. GPS: N34 21.339' / W84 39.375'

2.3 Turn right on the access trail to the Quarry Pond. GPS: N34 21.288' / W84 38.946'

3.7 Switchbacks lead to the high point of the West Loop Trail. GPS: N34 21.494' / W84 39.673'

3.9 The Ken Cannon Overlook offers a good winter vista. GPS: N34 21.389' / W84 39.666'

4.3 Close the loop at the West Loop Trail intersection. Retrace your steps to the end.

4.7 Return to the parking area.

Nearby Attractions

Funk Heritage Center at Reinhardt College, 7300 Reinhardt College Circle, Waleska 30183; (770) 720-5970; www.reinhardt.edu/funkheritage

26 Big Creek Greenway Trail

Located only a short distance from busy GA 400, the Big Creek Greenway offers a wooded retreat away from urban bustle and traffic. This section of the linear park is maintained by the city of Alpharetta and features a wide, paved pathway that follows the course of Big Creek for more than 8 miles as well as a 2.0-mile mountain-biking trail. The greenway trail is popular with hikers, runners, inline skaters, and bicyclists. The park also offers excellent sites for bird-watching and, occasionally, wildlife viewing (on a recent visit, we saw a white-tailed deer). The path also extends 1.5 miles west to Roswell's Big Creek Park; a noncontiguous 6.8-mile section of the Greenway has been developed in Forsyth County, with plans to link the sections and expand the system.

Start: Parking area off North Point Parkway
Distance: 6.6 miles point to point
Approximate hiking time: 2 to 3 hours (one way)
Elevation gain/loss: 37 feet
Trail surface: Concrete, wooden boardwalk, packed dirt (mountain-bike trail)
Lay of the land: Creek bottom, wetlands, and surrounding woods
Difficulty: Easy to moderate due to distance and level terrain
Seasons: Year-round

Other trail users: Bicyclists and inline skaters
Canine compatibility: Leashed dogs permitted
Land status: City of Alpharetta
Fees and permits: Free
Schedule: Open daily, 8 a.m. to dusk
Nearest town: Alpharetta
Maps: USGS Roswell; trail maps also available at the Alpharetta website
Trail contact: Alpharetta Recreation and Parks Department, 1825 Old Milton Pkwy., Alpharetta 30004; (678) 297-6123; http://alpharetta.ga.us

Finding the trailhead: Travel north on GA 400 to Mansell Road (exit 8). Turn right (east) on Mansell Road, then turn left (north) on North Point Parkway for 0.5 mile. On the right (east), just past an Ethan Allen furniture store, is the signed entrance for the greenway. There are additional parking areas at Haynes Bridge Road, Rock Mill Park off Kimball Bridge Road, and by the Ed Isakson YMCA off North Point Parkway. GPS: N34 02.784' / W84 17.744'

This is a linear trail. If you do not intend to retrace your steps to the starting point, you may wish to park a shuttle car at an end point or arrange for a pick-up.

The Hike

(*Note:* The greenway is marked with mileage signs at 0.5-mile increments. The signs mark the distance from the southern terminal point at Mansell Road to the northern terminus at Webb Bridge Road, a distance of 6.6 miles. The distances referenced in the hike description are based on beginning at the North Point parking area and following the loop trail south before continuing on the main trail to the north.)

Boardwalk trail south of main access trail

From the parking area off North Point Parkway, an access path winds past a comfort station for 0.2 mile to a three-way intersection with a bridge over Big Creek. Just before crossing the bridge, turn right and follow a narrow concrete path and wooden boardwalk along the western banks of Big Creek, then through a wetland area. At 0.6 mile, the trail bends left to an intersection with the main trail. A right turn leads to

Big Creek Greenway Trail

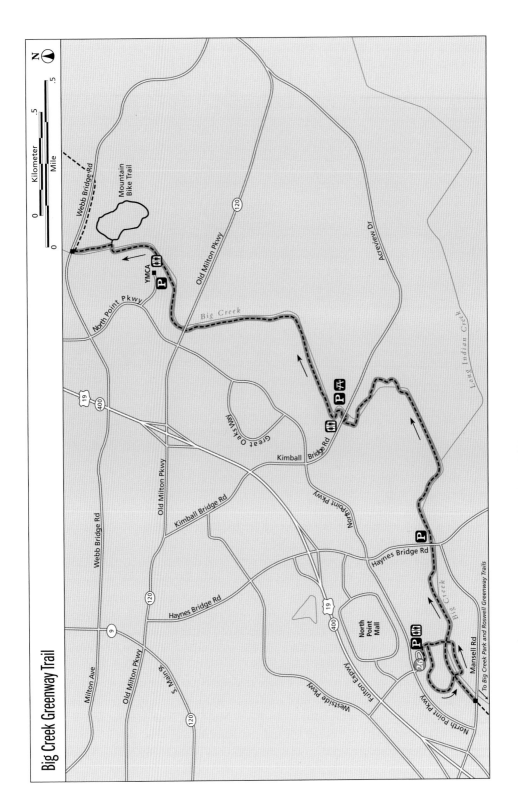

Paved Greenway path

Mansell Road; a left turn across a bridge closes the loop, returning you to the access path by the first bridge at about 0.9 mile.

Turn right and follow a wider cement path as it crosses a bridge and traces a northern route along Big Creek. A short distance ahead, another access trail exits to the right, leading to an office complex beyond the park boundary. Continue straight to a fork where the trail forms a short loop. Bear right and continue north. At 1.7 miles, the trail crosses beneath Haynes Bridge Road with an access trail to satellite parking on the left. Over the next half mile, the trail meanders closely by residential properties before crossing another bridge.

The trail passes an access trail to the right leading to Kimball Bridge Road before reaching an intersection with the same road at 3.5 miles. Turn right at the crosswalk and descend to the right as the path circles Rock Mill Park, with parking, restrooms, and picnic pavilions. The trail bends left and continues to follow the western banks of Big Creek. After crossing several bridges, the path goes beneath Old Milton Parkway (steps to the left lead to the road) before reaching a comfort station and parking area adjacent to the Ed Isakson YMCA building at 5.6 miles. This is the northernmost parking area on the greenway.

If you wish to continue to the greenway's northern terminus at Webb Bridge Road, bear right at the crosswalk and descend past the building to a level pathway. After crossing a bridge at 6.2 miles, the dirt mountain–bike trail exits the main path to the right. The greenway terminal point is ahead at 6.6 miles.

Miles and Directions

0.0 To begin, turn left past the information sign by the North Point Parkway parking area and hike east on the paved walkway. GPS: N34 02.784' / W84 17.744'

0.2 Reach a three-way intersection at the bridge over Big Creek. Just before crossing the bridge, turn right.

0.6 Take a left turn to cross the bridge.

0.9 Cross the bridge over Big Creek and turn right on the wider cement path of the greenway trail. GPS: N34 02.443' / W84 17.828'

1.7 The trail passes beneath Haynes Bridge Road. GPS: N34 02.533' / W84 17.076'

3.5 Turn right at the crosswalk to reach Rock Mill Park, with parking, restrooms, and picnic pavilions. GPS: N34 03.128' / W84 16.275'

5.3 Hike beneath the Old Milton Parkway Bridge. GPS: N34 04.045' / W84 15.589'

5.6 Pass the Ed Isakson YMCA, with a comfort station adjacent to the parking area. GPS: N34 04.173' / W84 15.197'

6.2 After crossing a bridge, the dirt mountain-bike trail exits the main path to the right.

6.6 Reach the end of the Alpharetta section of the greenway at Webb Bridge Road. GPS: N34 04.669' / W84 15.038'

27 Suwanee Creek Greenway Trail

Following the course of a slow-moving creek just east of Suwanee, this linear park meanders 4.7 miles, connecting multipurpose George Pierce Park in the north with Suwanee Creek Park in the south. A side trail near the greenway's midpoint leads to Town Center Park in the heart of Suwanee. An additional 0.7-mile soft-surface trail in Suwanee Creek Park provides hikers and bikers with a path along the Suwanee Creek floodplain, offering views of the creek and wetlands. Trail access is also available at Suwanee Sports Academy on Burnette Road, and at Martin Farm Park, about 0.5 mile west of Satellite Boulevard.

Start: Suwanee Creek Park or George Pierce Park
Distance: 4.7 miles point to point
Approximate hiking time: 2 hours
Elevation gain/loss: 135 feet
Trail surface: Asphalt, wooden boardwalks, compacted soil
Lay of the land: Gentle wooded hills and creek floodplain
Difficulty: Easy
Seasons: Year-round

Other trail users: Bicyclists and inline skaters
Canine compatibility: Leashed dogs permitted
Land status: City of Suwanee
Fees and permits: Free
Schedule: Open daily during daylight hours
Nearest town: Suwanee
Maps: USGS Suwanee; maps also available from the park website
Trail contact: City of Suwanee, 373 US 23 (Buford Highway), Suwanee 30024; (770) 945-8996; www.suwanee.com

Finding the trailhead: Drive north on I-85 to US 317, Lawrenceville-Suwanee Road (exit 111). Turn left (west) for 2 miles to Highway 13 (Buford Highway). Turn left (south) and drive through downtown Suwanee for 1.8 miles. The entrance to Suwanee Creek Park is on the left (east). Follow the entrance road for 0.1 mile to the parking area by the picnic pavilions and restroom building. GPS: N34 02.076' / W84 05.238'

You may also begin this hike at the northern terminus in George Pierce Park. To reach the George Pierce parking area, drive north on Buford Highway from US 317 for 0.2 mile and turn right (east) on the George Pierce Park entrance road. Travel 1.2 miles, past the community center and playground areas, to the parking lot at the northern end of the soccer complex. Park and cross the road, descending on the paved multiuse trail a short distance. At the bottom of the hill, recross the road and you will see an information sign at the trailhead. GPS: N 34 03.744' / W 84 02.635'

The Hike

The Suwanee Creek Greenway is a linear park connecting George Pierce and Suwanee Creek Parks, with ample parking at both locations, as well as on Martin Farm Road near the trail's midpoint. If you are hiking south to north, you may wish to leave a shuttle car in the large parking area at the northern end of Pierce Park's soccer complex, a short distance from the trail's end point.

Pathway along Suwanee Creek

The northbound route from Suwanee Creek Park is described. The trail begins at a plaza with information kiosk, comfort station, and picnic pavilion. Descend along a hillside contour and bear right toward busy Buford Highway. The trail climbs a ridge at 0.2 mile, crosses the park entrance road at 0.6 mile, then goes past the Buckeye picnic pavilion. The trail turns right and gently ascends to a ridge before turning sharply left and steadily descending toward Suwanee Creek.

A short distance above the floodplain turn right, past a sign noting passage through a native plant rescue area. Note the markers identifying various plants, including American holly, foamflower, Callaway ginger, and native azalea. At 0.9 mile, the trail

Trail near Buckeye Pavilion

reaches the floodplain and follows a level boardwalk over a wetlands area. To the right is your first glimpse of Suwanee Creek.

After crossing a second boardwalk, the trail passes through a marsh area with a shallow pond to the right of the path. At 1.6 miles, the trail reaches McGinnis Ferry Road with a parking area off Burnette Road behind commercial buildings. At the trail information sign, the path descends to the right, and then goes sharply left beneath the McGinnis Ferry Road Bridge. On the far side, the path ascends to the left and crosses the bridge along the sidewalk, rejoining the greenway on the eastern side of Suwanee Creek.

From the bridge, the trail descends on a boardwalk switchback to the creek and continues north, crossing beneath a covered canopy at 1.9 miles. After cresting a ridge and bending to the right, the path descends to the left returning to the creek floodplain at 2.2 miles.

Suwanee Creek was once known as "Black Branch" for the toxic sediments flushed into the waters by the Bona Allen Tannery, which operated upstream for nearly a century. When the tannery closed in the early 1970s, aggressive efforts were undertaken to restore the creek. Today, aquatic animals and plants have returned to the creek's clear waters.

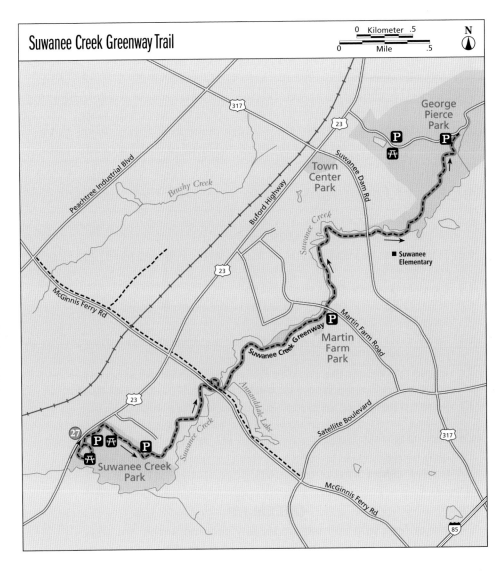

Suwanee Creek Greenway Trail

Beyond a dead-end road on the right, the greenway follows a wetlands board-walk then reaches open meadows south of Martin Farm Road. Along this section are several signed observation areas describing Suwanee Creek and notable birds and wildlife that may be seen. Cross the road, and follow the narrowed path as it continues north through an open area surrounded by woods.

At 3.4 miles, an elevated pedestrian path exits to the right, then crosses over the main trail. This side path leads about 0.4 mile along Suwanee Dam Road (US 317) to Town Center Park. Continue straight, crossing beneath the road and follow the Richard Trice Trail (a wooden boardwalk) for about 0.1 mile before merging with the paved trail.

At 3.7 miles the trail forks, with a paved path continuing to the right toward Suwanee Elementary School. Take the bridge to the left and cross Suwanee Creek. Turn right on a dirt trail that reenters a heavily wooded area.

At 4.0 miles, trails from George Pierce Park intersect from the left, and a short distance beyond is a bridge over a wetlands area. Cross the bridge and follow the dirt trail as it follows rolling hills, bending left above a large meadow on the right.

At 4.7 miles the trail ends near the northern terminus of George Pierce Park's main road. Cross the road and follow the paved trail uphill to the left to reach a parking area beside the park's soccer complex.

Miles and Directions

0.0 The paved trail begins to the right of the restrooms at the Suwanee Creek Park parking area. GPS: N34 02.076' / W84 05.238'

0.6 The trail crosses the entrance road by the Buckeye picnic pavilion. GPS: N34 02.157' / W84 05.064'

1.0 Two wooden boardwalks cross a wetlands area.

1.6 At the trail information sign, bear right and then walk beneath the McGinnis Ferry Road Bridge. GPS: N34 02.351' / W84 04.547'

2.3 The trail bends left at the road intersection. Cross a long boardwalk before reaching a meadow south of Martin Farm Road.

3.4 The path to Town Center Park exits to the right and then bends left, crossing above the Suwanee Creek Greenway Trail over the road bridge. GPS: N34 03.064' / W84 03.640'

3.7 Bear left as the trail forks, crossing an elevated boardwalk. The path to the right leads to Suwanee Elementary School. GPS: N34 03.067' / W84 03.362'

4.0 Follow the boardwalk and bridge over a wetlands area. GPS: N34 03.237' / W84 03.232'

4.7 Reach the end of the trail at George Pierce Park Road. Turn left and follow a paved path up to the parking area by the soccer fields. GPS: N 34 03.744' / W 84 02.635'

GREEN TIP

Never feed wild animals under any circumstances. You may damage their health and expose yourself (and them) to danger.

28 Sawnee Mountain Preserve: Indian Seats Trails

Set on 963 acres just north of Cumming, the Sawnee Mountain Preserve provides a passive greenspace with picnic shelters, a playground, a comfort station, an out-door amphitheater, a visitor center, and a network of foot trails along the slopes of 1,963-foot-high Sawnee Mountain. The Forsyth County Park opened to hikers in 2005. Sawnee Mountain Preserve offers more than 11 miles of trails along slopes and over a mountain summit. The Visitor Center opened at the preserve's northern entrance in 2008. The Indian Seats Trail system follows the slopes of Sawnee Mountain to Indian Seats, a rock outcrop at the summit, on a series of connecting loops.

Start: Parking area
Distance: 4.4-mile circuit
Approximate hiking time: 2 to 3 hours
Elevation gain/loss: 597 feet
Trail surface: Compacted soil
Lay of the land: Wooded slopes and exposed mountain summit
Difficulty: Moderate
Seasons: Year-round
Canine compatibility: Dogs not permitted
Land status: Forsyth County Parks and Recreation
Fees and permits: Free

Schedule: Open daily, 6 a.m. to dark. The visitor center is open from 8:30 a.m. to 5 p.m. Mon to Sat. It is closed for Thanksgiving, Christmas Eve/Christmas Day, and New Year's Day.
Nearest town: Cumming
Maps: USGS Matt and Cumming; map also available at the park and on the Forsyth County website
Trail contact: Forsyth County Parks and Recreation Department, PO Box 2417, Cumming 30040; (770) 781-2217; www.forsythco.com. Park maps feature numbered markers that coincide with diamond-shaped signs on the trails.

Finding the trailhead: Travel north on GA 400 to Bald Ridge Marina Road (exit 15). Travel west 1.2 miles to downtown Cumming and turn right (north) on Tribble Gap Road (the name soon changes to Bettis-Tribble Gap Road). Drive north 3.0 miles; the entrance to Sawnee Mountain Preserve's Indian Seats Trails system is on the right (east) at 2500 Bettis-Tribble Gap Rd. To reach the Visitor Center, continue north on Bettis-Tribble Gap Road for 1.6 miles to Spot Road. Turn right (east) and drive 0.4 mile to the north entrance to the preserve at 4075 Spot Rd. GPS: N34 14.702' / W84 08.334'

The Hike

From the south parking area, follow the Indian Seats Trail that begins behind the comfort station, playground, and picnic pavilions. The path gently descends to the right and bends east past an informational marker describing the area's colorful gold mining history (you will see evidence of mining pits and tunnels along the trail).

Sawnee Mountain summit rock outcrops

Ascend on a series of switchbacks, passing the intersection with the Yucca Trail entering from the left. Continue a moderate but steady climb on long switchbacks to the area of exposed rock dubbed "Indian Seats," located just below the mountain's summit at 1.0 mile. An informational marker notes the possible ceremonial use of this site by Native Americans centuries ago. To the right, you may climb among the rocks on a short side trail to reach a wooden observation platform offering a panoramic view of surrounding woodlands and meadows, and beyond to the southern peaks of the Appalachian Mountains.

Along Indian Seats Trail

Retrace your steps from the summit, past Indian Seats, and bear right as the trail gently descends along the southwestern slope of the mountain. In winter, leafless trees open up wide vistas of the slopes and surrounding foothills to the south.

Continuing to descend on switchbacks, reach an intersection with the Laurel Trail. The Indian Seats Trail bends to the left on a return toward the trailhead, but this hike continues toward the northwest on the Laurel Trail, making a moderate to steep descent through stands of its namesake mountain laurel.

As you approach the base of Sawnee Mountain at 2.3 miles, the Laurel Trail bends sharply left, and the Northern Access Trail continues straight, leading a short distance

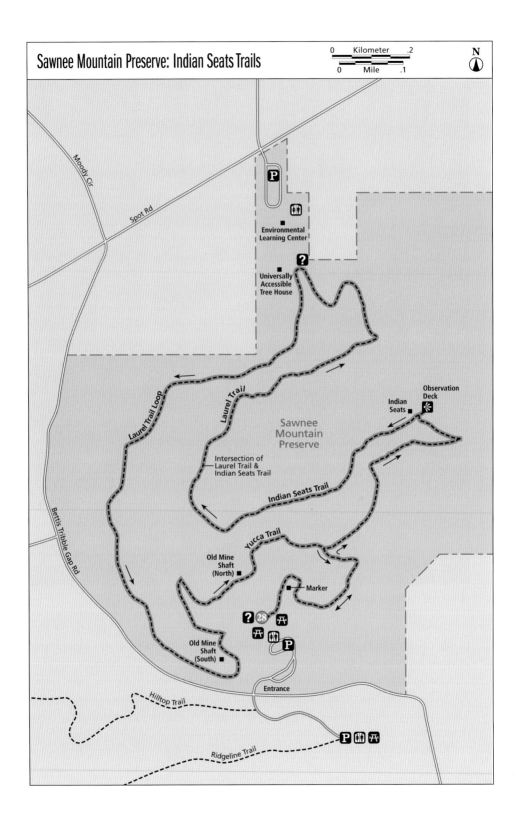

Sawnee Mountain Preserve: Indian Seats Trails

Moody Cir

Spot Rd

P

Environmental
Learning Center

Universally
Accessible
Tree House

?

Laurel Trail Loop

Laurel Trail

Sawnee
Mountain
Preserve

Indian
Seats

Observation
Deck

Intersection of
Laurel Trail &
Indian Seats Trail

Indian Seats Trail

Bettis Tribble Gap Rd

Yucca Trail

Old Mine
Shaft
(North)

Marker

? 28

Old Mine
Shaft
(South)

P

Entrance

Hilltop Trail

P

Ridgeline Trail

N

0   Kilometer   .2
0   Mile   .1

ATOP INDIAN SEATS

The mountain draws its name from Sawnee, a Cherokee Indian chief who welcomed early-nineteenth-century settlers into the area around what is modern-day Cumming. Historical evidence suggests that an outcrop of rock atop the mountain, now called Indian Seats, may have served ceremonial purposes for early Native Americans who occupied this area more than 1,000 years ago. Within the last century, the mountain slopes were mined for gold, and evidence of miners' pits and tunnels may still be seen within the preserve.

to the Visitor Center and north parking area. If time permits, tour the interactive exhibits in the center before returning to the Laurel Trail to complete your hike.

From the visitor center, turn right on the Laurel Trail and steadily ascend along the western slope of the mountain. After cresting a shallow ridge, descend past an old, gated mine tunnel as you approach the Tribble Gap Road parking area. A short distance ahead, the trail to the parking area continues straight, and the Laurel Trail bends sharply left and steeply ascends. Following the Laurel Trail, you soon reach a T intersection with the Indian Seats Trail at 3.5 miles.

Turn left and follow the Indian Seats Trail as it ascends to an intersection with the western head of the Yucca Trail. Turn right and follow the Yucca Trail as it traverses the southern slope of the mountain, passing another gated mine shaft visible to the left of the path. At the eastern terminus of the trail, turn right and retrace your steps on the Indian Seats Trail, returning to the south parking area at 4.4 miles.

Miles and Directions

0.0 The access trail climbs a short distance from the south parking area to the Indian Seats Trail. GPS: N34 14.702' / W84 08.334'

0.5 Pass the intersection with the Yucca Trail to the left. Bend to the right and remain on the Indian Seats Trail. GPS: N34 14.822' / W84 08.259'

1.0 Just below the mountain's summit, you reach the Indian Seats rock outcrops. A short trail ascends to a wooden observation platform with panoramic views. GPS: N34 15.012' / W84 08.107'

1.6 At the intersection of Indian Seats and Laurel Trails, continue straight on the Laurel Trail. GPS: N34 14.942' / W84 08.457'

2.3 Turn left at the intersection of the Laurel Trail and the North Access Trail to the Visitor Learning Center. GPS: N34 15.165' / W84 08.253'

3.3 Pass the entrance to a gated old gold-mine shaft, and bend sharply left on the Laurel Trail.

3.5 Turn left on Indian Seats Trail from the Laurel Trail. GPS: N34 14.710' / W84 08.416'

3.6 Turn right and ascend on the Yucca Trail. GPS: N34 14.806' / W84 08.484'

4.0 Turn right at the Indian Seats Trail intersection.

4.4 Return to the south parking area by the restrooms, playground, and picnic pavilions.

29 Sawnee Mountain Preserve: Mountainside Trails

Sawnee Mountain Preserve's Mountainside Trail system opened in 2016 on land acquired by Forsyth County in the mid-2000s. While the trails in this section do not offer panoramic views of the surrounding countryside and Appalachian Mountain foothills, they provide a scenic hike through a southern oak and hickory forest. The Mountainside Trails system is composed of two connected loops formed by the Ridgeline, Mountainside, and Hilltop Trails.

Start: Parking area with picnic pavilions and comfort station
Distance: 5.2-mile circuit
Approximate hiking time: 2 to 3 hours
Elevation gain/loss: 503 feet
Trail surface: Compacted soil
Lay of the land: Wooded slopes and rocky terrain
Difficulty: Moderate
Seasons: Year-round
Canine compatibility: Dogs not permitted
Land status: Forsyth County Parks and Recreation
Fees and permits: Free

Schedule: Open daily, 6 a.m. to dark. The visitor center is open from 8:30 a.m. to 5 p.m., Mon to Sat. It is closed for Thanksgiving, Christmas Eve/Christmas Day, and New Year's Day.
Nearest town: Cumming
Maps: USGS Matt and Cumming; map also available at the park and on the Forsyth County website. Park maps feature numbered markers that coincide with diamond-shaped signs on the trails.
Trail contact: Forsyth County Parks and Recreation Department, PO Box 2417, Cumming 30040; (770) 781-2217; www.forsythco.com.

Finding the trailhead: Drive north on GA 400 to Bald Ridge Marina Road (exit 15). Travel west 1.2 miles to downtown Cumming and turn right (north) on Tribble Gap Road (the name soon changes to Bettis-Tribble Gap Road). Drive north 3.0 miles; the entrance to Sawnee Mountain Preserve's Mountainside Trails is on the left (west) at 2505 Bettis-Tribble Gap Rd. To reach the Visitor Center, continue north on Bettis-Tribble Gap Road for 1.6 miles to Spot Road. Turn right (east) and drive 0.4 mile to the north entrance to the preserve at 4075 Spot Rd. GPS: N34 14.504' / W84 08.190'

The Hike

From the west side of the parking area follow the Ridgeline Trail, located by the picnic pavilion, playground, and comfort station. The trail enters the woods and begins a moderate ascent along the spine of a series of east-west ridges.

At 1.0 mile, reach the intersection with the Mountainside Trail and follow the level path to the left. In a short distance, the trail begins a steep climb to a sharp left switchback and continues ascending to a stair crossing of Tower Road at 1.5 miles.

Along the blue-blazed Mountainside Trail

Bear left and continue the ascent before a sharp right turn and a gradual descent along the southern slope.

After a series of switchbacks along rolling terrain, turn left and descend along an old roadbed, reaching the intersection of the Church Trail (satellite parking access) at 2.2 miles. Continue descending along a rocky stretch of the Mountainside Trail as it bends right and takes a northeasterly path along the northern slopes of the mountain. After a series of long, undulating, and at times steep ascents and descents along the slope, the path reaches the intersection with the Hilltop Trail at 3.8 miles. The path to the right is the connector to the Ridgeline Trail.

Follow the Hilltop Trail straight as it descends on a series of switchbacks to a small pond (accessible by a short side trail). Bear right at a split-rail fence marking the preserve boundary, and follow a moderate ascent along the north slope of the ridge, reaching a level area at 4.7 miles. Continue on a gradual descent back to the parking area at 5.2 miles.

Sawnee Mountain Preserve: Mountainside Trails

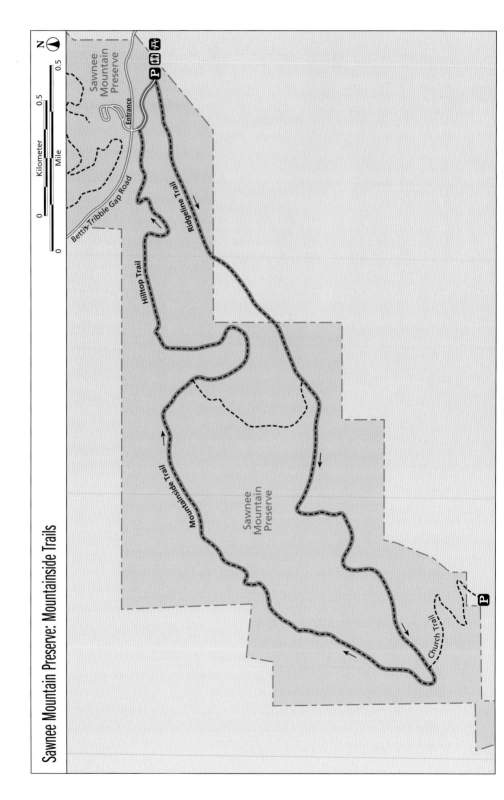

Bettis Tribble Gap Road

Entrance

Sawnee Mountain Preserve

Hilltop Trail

Ridgeline Trail

Mountainside Trail

Sawnee Mountain Preserve

Church Trail

Kilometer

Mile

N

Autumn foliage along Mountainside Trail

Miles and Directions

0.0 Begin the ascent along the Ridgeline Trail from the parking area. GPS: N34 14.504' / W84 08.190'

1.0 Reach the intersection with Mountainside Trail. Continue on the Mountainside Trail. GPS: N34 14.236' / W84 08.831'

1.5 Cross Tower Road. GPS: N34 14.119' / W84 09.409'

2.2 Reach the intersection of the Mountainside and Church Trails.

3.8 Arrive at the intersection of the Mountainside and Hilltop Trails. Continue on the Hilltop Trail. GPS: N34 14.374' / W84 09.203'

5.2 Return to the parking area and trailhead.

30 Elachee Nature Science Center at Chicopee Woods Nature Preserve

Elachee Nature Science Center serves as an environmental education component of the 1,440-acre Chicopee Woods Nature Preserve, established by the city of Gainesville in 1978. Several short trail loops meander through the upper piedmont foothills surrounding the science center, while longer paths descend along wooded slopes to Chicopee Lake and Elachee's Aquatic Studies Center. The hike described here traces a loop through forested hills and wetlands areas surrounding the lake.

Start: Lake Trail parking area near the nature center

Distance: 6.4 miles on interconnected loops

Approximate hiking time: 3 to 4 hours

Elevation gain/loss: 200 feet

Trail surface: Soft packed dirt and clay

Lay of the land: Wooded slopes, wetlands, and lakeshore

Difficulty: Moderate to difficult due to distance and steep terrain

Seasons: Year-round

Canine compatibility: Dogs not permitted on trails Mon through Fri. Leashed dogs permitted on Sat and Sun.

Land status: Chicopee Woods Area Park Commission; private, nonprofit (Elachee Nature Science Center)

Fees and permits: Daily parking fee; annual pass for Chicopee Woods access. Nature science center admission is also charged.

Schedule: Open daily from 7 a.m. to dusk; nature science center is open 10 a.m. to 5 p.m. Mon through Sat from March through November; 10 a.m. to 3 p.m. from December through February

Nearest town: Gainesville

Maps: USGS Chestnut Mountain; trail maps also available at the nature center and on the park website.

Trail contact: Elachee Nature Science Center, 2125 Elachee Dr., Gainesville 30504; (770) 535-1976; www.elachee.org

Finding the trailhead: Follow I-85 north to I-985 (exit 113). Travel north on I-985 for 16 miles to GA 53 (exit 16). Turn right (east) on Mundy Mill Road/GA 53, then left (north) at the second traffic light on Atlanta Highway/Highway 13. Drive north for 4.0 miles, over I-985 and past Chicopee Woods Golf Course, then turn right (east) on Elachee Drive (note the sign for Chicopee Woods Nature Preserve and Elachee Nature Center). The road bends sharply right (south), then left (east), crosses I-985, and ends at the nature center parking area. The hike begins a short distance from the nature center at the Lake Trails parking area. There is a satellite parking area at Chicopee Lake off Calvary Church Road. GPS: N34 14.644' / W83 49.995'

The Hike

From the Lake Trails parking area west of the nature center, the trail enters the woods past an information board. A short distance ahead, turn right and descend along the pink-blazed Dunlap Trail through mixed forest, highlighted by mountain laurel and

Suspension bridge over Walnut Creek

several ancient white oaks, before crossing the Homestead Creek bottomland, lush with ferns.

Climb away from the creek, following the slope and passing a sign noting entry into the neotropical migratory bird conservation area. After descending, cross the Walnut Creek suspension bridge at 1.4 miles and follow the Dunlap Trail as it curves along the creek and gradually climbs to an intersection with the orange-blazed East Lake Trail at 1.8 miles.

Turn sharply right and follow the East Lake Trail, descending steadily on several long switchbacks to a wetlands area. As you climb the shallow hills on the far side, cross two footbridges over small streams before turning left and exiting the woods at 2.7 miles. A short walk to the right leads to the Chicopee Lake Aquatic Studies Center, with picnic pavilion, lakeside deck, and satellite parking area.

Begin your return hike by crossing the lake's earthen dam on the Rod Smith Birding Trail (named in memory of a local naturalist) before reentering the woods and merging with the orange-blazed West Lake Trail. A short distance ahead, at 3.1

Trail above Chicopee Lake

miles, the Pine Grove Loop Trail forks to the left and climbs along wooded slopes before rejoining the main path; after a quick descent to a curving wetlands boardwalk, the trail climbs to a vista point above the lake. Continue on the West Lake Trail as it follows a meandering course through lowland forests, reaching the Walnut Creek suspension bridge at 4.7 miles.

The preserve is a National Audubon Society Important Bird Area, reflecting its significance as a habitat for nesting and migratory bird species. In addition, the US Forest Service has designated portions of the preserve as permanent monitoring areas for the neotropical migratory bird conservation program.

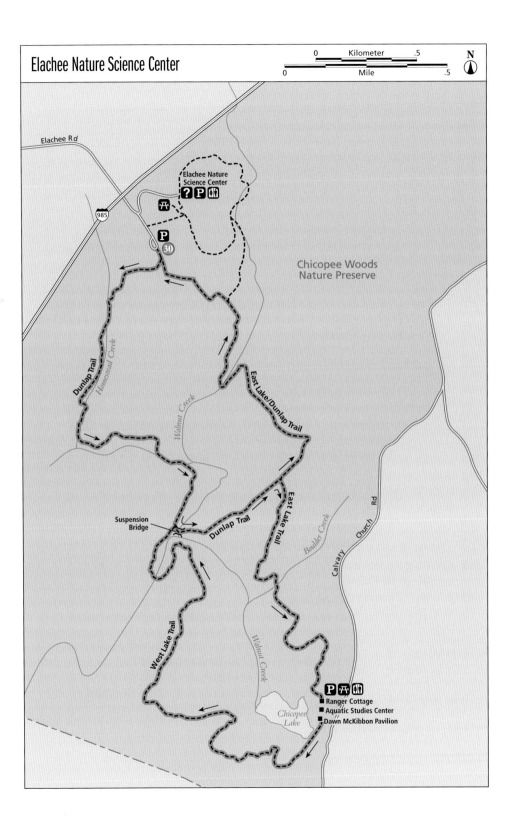

Elachee Nature Science Center

Elachee Rd

985

Elachee Nature
Science Center

? P

Chicopee Woods
Nature Preserve

P
30

Dunlap Trail

Homestead Creek

Walnut Creek

East Lake/Dunlap Trail

Suspension
Bridge

Dunlap Trail

East Lake Trail

Boulder Creek

Calvary Church Rd

West Lake Trail

Walnut Creek

Chicopee Lake

P

■ Ranger Cottage
■ Aquatic Studies Center
■ Dawn McKibbon Pavilion

0   Kilometer   .5
0   Mile   .5

N

Retrace your steps across the bridge, back up the Dunlap Creek Trail, and past the intersection with the East Lake Trail. Continue steadily climbing north on the combined Dunlap/East Lake Trail toward the nature science center.

After crossing a ridge and steeply descending to a small footbridge across Walnut Creek, the trail forks, with the Dunlap/East Lake Trail bending to the right and the Walnut Creek Trail winding away to the left. Continue on the Dunlap/East Lake Trail as it ascends, at times steeply, to an intersection with the Mathis Trail at 6.2 miles. Turn left on the blue-blazed Mathis Trail. At the Mathis Connector Trail intersection, turn left. The trail ends at the West Lake Trail. A right turn will return you to the parking area at 6.4 miles.

If you wish to extend your explorations, the Ed Dodd and Geiger Trails are shorter paths that loop around the nature center and connect with the Elachee Trail system.

Miles and Directions

0.0 From the southern end of the Lake Trails parking area by the information kiosk, hike south for a short distance. Follow the Dunlap Trail to the right. GPS: N34 14.644' / W83 49.995'

0.7 Cross a footbridge over Homestead Creek. GPS: N34 14.217' / W83 50.050'

1.4 Turn left and cross the suspension bridge over Walnut Creek. GPS: N34 14.067' / W83 49.886'

1.8 Turn right on the East Lake Trail. GPS: N34 14.132' / W83 49.635'

2.2 Use the footbridge to cross Boulder Creek.

2.7 Pause on the observation deck at the Chicopee Lake Aquatic Studies Center. GPS: N34 13.622' / W83 49.514'

3.1 Take the left to follow the short Pine Grove Loop before reconnecting to the West Lake Trail.

3.6 Reach the lake overlook with benches that offer a good spot for birding.

4.6 Cross a footbridge over the wetlands area and bear to the right. GPS: N34 13.944' / W83 49.968'

4.7 Retrace your steps over the suspension bridge along Dunlap Trail.

5.3 Continue straight at the intersection with East Lake Trail.

6.2 Turn left at the intersection with Mathis Trail to the Mathis Connector Trail. GPS: N 34 14.585' /W 83 49.754'

6.3 Turn left at the Mathis Connector Trail.

6.4 Reach the West Lake Trail and turn right for a short hike to the Lake Trails parking area.

Events

Great Backyard Bird Count, February; Stars over Elachee, monthly
Information on these and other events: www.elachee.org; (770) 535-1976

Nearby Attractions

Northeast Georgia History Center, 322 Academy St., Gainesville 30503; (770) 297-5900; www.negahc.org

31 Little Mulberry Park Trails

Nestled in the northeastern corner of Gwinnett County, Little Mulberry Park is an 892-acre greenspace featuring more than 13 miles of hiking, biking, and equestrian paths meandering across meadows, through the 200-acre Karina Miller Nature Preserve, and around Miller Lake. In addition to recreational facilities, Little Mulberry Park also preserves trace evidence of early Native American habitation in mysterious "stone mounds" found along sections of the 2.2-mile Ravine Loop Trail. The hike profiled in this chapter begins at the southern parking area and includes a walk along the paved Meadows Trails, Ravine Trail, Carriage Trail, and Miller Lake Trail.

Start: Southern parking area off Fence Road
Distance: 8.3 miles of interconnecting loops
Approximate hiking time: 3 to 4 hours
Elevation gain/loss: 316 feet
Trail surface: Asphalt and compacted soil
Lay of the land: Open meadows, heavily wooded slopes, creek bottoms
Difficulty: Moderate to strenuous due to distance and occasionally steep terrain
Seasons: Year-round
Other trail users: Bicyclists and inline skaters on paved trails; equestrians on designated trails

Canine compatibility: Leashed dogs permitted
Land status: Gwinnett County Parks and Recreation
Fees and permits: Free
Nearest town: Auburn
Maps: USGS Hog Mountain and Auburn; maps also available at the park and on the Gwinnett County website
Trail contact: Little Mulberry Park, 3855 Fence Rd., Auburn 30011; (770) 978-5270; www.gwinnettcounty.com

Finding the trailhead: Travel north on I-85 to Hamilton Mill Road (exit 120). Turn right (south) on Hamilton Mill for 0.1 mile and turn right (west) on GA 124 (Braselton Highway). Follow the highway for 1.9 miles to GA 324 (Auburn Highway) and turn left (east). Drive 3.4 miles and turn left (east) on Fence Road. The park entrance is 0.6 mile ahead on the left. GPS: N34 02.281' / W83 52.631'

Parking for the northern end of the park is located on Hog Mountain Road. It can be reached by turning left (south) from GA 124 on Hog Mountain Church Road, then left (east) again on Hog Mountain Road. Drive about 2.2 miles to the park entrance on the right. GPS: N34 02.358' / W83 52.657'

The Hike

From the plaza above the south parking area, turn left past an information kiosk and picnic pavilion on the West Meadow Trail. Ascend a long switchback to the left, reaching the Ravine Trail at 0.3 mile. Turn left through an arbor with a trail map and enter deep woods on a mulch trail. Soon the trail steeply descends, crossing bridges over intermittent streams, before reaching an intersection at 0.5 mile. A short distance

Overlook on Ravine Loop Trail

ahead, a spur overlook trail offers views of a lush ravine set deep beneath a canopy of hardwoods. A round-trip along the spur trail adds 0.5 mile to the hike.

Retrace your steps to the intersection, turn right on the Ravine Trail, and follow a gradually descending path above the ravine. The trail soon bends right, reaching the intersection with a side trail at 1.5 miles. Ahead, notice a sign describing the mysterious stacked stones visible in the nearby woods (and elsewhere). The path then descends, at times steeply along steps, to a creek valley at 1.9 miles. Here you bend right and follow the creek for about 0.3 mile before climbing away from the water to a wooden bridge over a stream at 2.3 miles. Beyond the bridge, the trail ascends

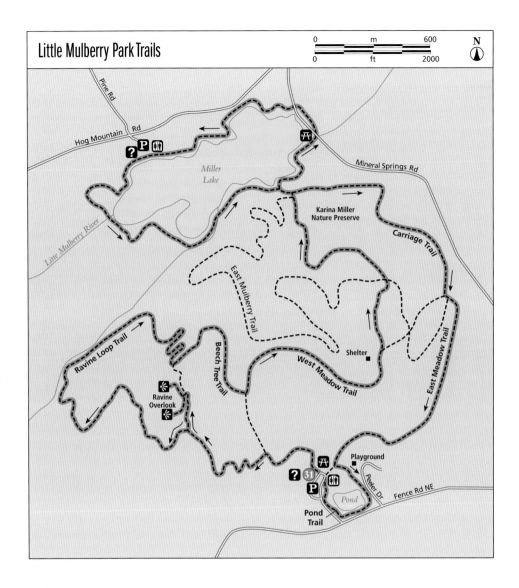

Little Mulberry Park Trails

0   m   600
0   ft   2000

N

Pine Rd

Hog Mountain Rd

Miller Lake

Mineral Springs Rd

Little Mulberry River

Karina Miller Nature Preserve

Carriage Trail

East Mulberry Trail

Ravine Loop Trail

Beech Tree Trail

Ravine Overlook

West Meadow Trail

Shelter

East Meadow Trail

Playground

31

Peeler Dr

Pond

Fence Rd NE

Pond Trail

on stepped switchbacks to the Beech Tree Trail at 2.5 miles. Turn left (the straight trail leads to the ravine overlook), and climb back to West Meadow Trail at 2.9 miles.

Turn left and follow the paved trail along the meadow's edge, then descend past a picnic pavilion to a four-way intersection at 3.5 miles. Bear left on the East Meadow Trail to the intersection with the Carriage Trail. Follow the Carriage Trail as it descends to a crossing of the East Mulberry Trail at 3.7 miles. A short distance ahead, a sign marks the boundary of the Karina Miller Nature Preserve. The Carriage Trail soon follows a sharp switchback before reaching a second intersection with the East Mulberry Trail. Cross two bridges over a small creek and join the Miller Lake Loop Trail at 4.1 miles, bearing right along the lake shore.

Stone cairns on Ravine Loop Trail

At 4.3 miles, the trail bends left and crosses an earthen dam. On the far side, the path meanders through a meadow area, bending right and descending closer to the water. At 5.0 miles, a short side trail leads to a pier and small boat launch. Continue on the lake trail as it ascends past the access trail to the Hog Mountain Road parking area at 5.3 miles. Descend along the water's edge, reaching a small pier and picnic area at 5.5 miles. Here, the trail makes a sharp "horseshoe" turn through a wetlands area before reentering the nature preserve at 6.0 miles.

After completing the Miller Lake Trail at 6.3 miles, turn right on the Carriage Trail for a short distance before turning left on the East Mulberry Trail as it climbs past the equestrian access trail and through the nature preserve. The trail ascends more steeply along a series of switchbacks before exiting the woods and intersecting with the East Meadow Trail at 7.0 miles. Turn left and follow the paved trail as it descends through the meadow, bearing right on a return toward the plaza.

Shortly before reaching the starting point, take a short connecting path on the left linking to the paved, ADA-accessible Pond Trail. Wind past a large playground and around a small pond near the park entrance. After circling the pond, the path ascends past a picnic pavilion to the starting point at 8.3 miles.

Miles and Directions

0.0 Start by passing the information kiosk on the plaza; turn left on the West Meadow Trail. GPS: N34 02.358' / W83 52.657'

0.3 Turn left on the Ravine Trail. GPS: N34 02.450' / W83 52.786'

1.9 Below the site of the stone mounds, the trail bends sharply to the right at the creek bottom area. GPS: N34 02.615' / W83 53.450'

2.5 Turn left on Beech Tree Trail. GPS: N34 02.630' / W83 53.083'

2.9 Rejoin the paved West Meadow Trail. GPS: N34 02.558' / W83 52.857'

3.5 At the four-way intersection, turn left on East Meadow Trail.

3.7 Continue straight on the Carriage Trail. GPS: N34 02.667' / W83 52.535'

4.1 The Carriage Trail reaches two footbridges. Continue straight to the Miller Lake Loop Trail.

4.3 Cross an earthen dam impounding Miller Lake. GPS: N34 03.219' / W83 52.678'

5.3 Pass the intersection with the access trail to Hog Mountain Road parking area. GPS: N34 03.204' / W83 53.080'

6.0 Reenter the Karina Miller Nature Preserve.

6.3 Turn right on the Carriage Trail for a short distance, then turn left on the East Mulberry Trail. GPS: N34 02.975' / W83 52.821'

7.0 Turn left onto the paved East Meadow Trail. GPS: N34 02.802' / W83 52.289'

7.7 Bear left on the short connecting path that links to the paved, ADA-accessible Pond Trail by the playground.

8.3 Complete the loop around the pond and return to the starting point by the picnic pavilion.

Nearby Attractions

Chateau Elan Winery and Resort, 100 Rue Charlemagne, Braselton 30517; (678) 425-0900; www.chateauelan.com

32 State Botanical Garden of Georgia

Set aside by the University of Georgia in 1968, the 313-acre gardens complex includes the glass-enclosed visitor center, the stone-and-timber Day Chapel, the Callaway classroom building, the Alice H. Richards Children's Garden, and the Garden Club of Georgia headquarters. In addition to paths through specialty gardens of native and exotic plants and herbs, the botanical garden features more than 7 miles of trails in the surrounding forests, wetlands, and floodplains of the Middle Oconee River. The state botanical garden serves multiple purposes, including use as a "living laboratory" for university instruction and research, as well as a destination for hikers and wildlife watchers.

Start: Plaza in front of the visitor center
Distance: 4.9-mile loop
Approximate hiking time: 3 hours
Elevation gain/loss: 166 feet
Trail surface: Compacted soil, gravel, short paved sections
Lay of the land: Upland forests, slopes, wetlands, and floodplains
Difficulty: Moderate
Seasons: Year-round
Canine compatibility: Dogs not permitted
Land status: University of Georgia

Fees and permits: Free (donations encouraged and memberships available)
Schedule: Gardens open daily from 8 a.m. to 6 p.m. (8 p.m. in summer); visitor center and conservatory open 9 a.m. to 4:30 p.m. Tues through Sat, 11:30 a.m. to 4:30 p.m. Sun; closed Mon
Nearest town: Athens
Maps: USGS Athens West; maps also available at the conservatory
Trail contact: State Botanical Garden of Georgia, 2450 South Milledge Ave., Athens 30605; (706) 542-1244; www.botgarden.uga.edu

Finding the trailhead: Drive north on I-85 to GA 316 (exit 106). Follow GA 316 for 40 miles to the intersection with US 78/GA 10 (South Bypass); turn right (east). At 4.6 miles, exit the bypass and turn right (south) on South Milledge Avenue. Travel for 2 miles and the gardens entrance is on the right. GPS: N33 54.135' / W83 23.027'

The Hike

From the conservatory plaza, cross the small parking area and descend to the right through the pleasant Shade Garden on paved switchbacks. Cross a service road and make a short ascent as the White Trail follows a rolling course past the Annual/Perennial and Trial garden beds before descending into woods.

The trail climbs to a ridge at 0.6 mile, reaching a fence and deer gate. Cross through the gate and gently descend. At the intersection with the Red Trail, bear right, remaining on the White Trail, descending more steeply to a footbridge across an intermittent stream. Cross and hike through a lush bottomland area before climbing the opposite slope, reaching a power-line corridor at 0.9 mile.

White Trail along Middle Oconee River

Reenter the woods on the opposite side of the corridor and follow an easy descent to a footbridge over another intermittent stream. Climb a long switchback to a ridge crest at 1.2 miles before descending the slopes and continuing to the outermost point of the White Trail. The path bends sharply left and follows a narrow stream valley, crossing several footbridges, before crossing the power-line corridor again at 1.7 miles.

In the woods on the opposite side of the power line, the path descends on switchbacks past a deep ravine to the right of the trail, reaching a creek bottom at 2.1 miles. Cross a small bridge and ascend past a first intersection with the Red Trail, reaching the second intersection with the Red Trail at 2.4 miles. Continue climbing to an intersection with the Green Trail, by a covered shelter with information board and map. Turn right, remaining on the White Trail, and descend on a long switchback, passing an intersection with the Blue Trail, with a sharp bend to the left above the Middle Oconee River at 2.8 miles.

The trail follows the riverbank and floodplain, passing an informational sign about a collaborative project of the university and the US Forest Service to address Chinese

White blaze along wooded path

privet and other invasive plant species. Continue to follow the river, reaching a footbridge over a river tributary at 3.4 miles, a short distance from another crossing of the power-line corridor. At this point, the White Trail becomes the Orange Trail and continues along the riverbank.

After passing an intersection with the Orange Alternate Trail, the path crosses a footbridge past a marsh area. The trail bends sharply left, away from the river, and curves along the edge of the marsh before beginning a gentle climb along a streambed and into wooded hills. Note informational signs describing the evidence of agricultural use and forest succession along the trail.

State Botanical Garden of Georgia

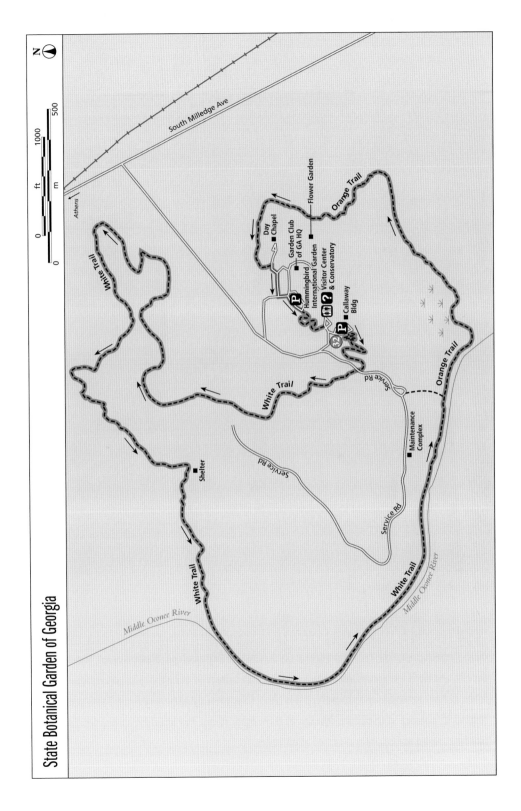

Path through Shade Garden

During your visit to the botanical gardens, spend time strolling through the numerous specialty gardens, including the International Garden, Native Flora Garden, Shade Garden, Flower Garden, and Heritage Garden. Also, don't miss the rich collection of lush tropical plants found in the visitor center and conservatory. If it is open, take a few minutes to visit the Day Chapel (named in memory of Cecil Day, founder of Days Inns) to see the beautiful stonework and skillfully carved mahogany and etched glass doors.

Pass a footbridge and access trail, continuing on the Orange Trail. At 4.2 miles, cross another footbridge, noting evidence of storm-downed trees in the surrounding woods. After a steady ascent, pass through the fence and deer gate and reenter the main gardens area. Continue climbing, reaching the trail terminus at 4.6 miles. At this point, you may cross the parking area, past the Garden Club of Georgia headquarters, and follow the Hummingbird Trail (brochures available in the visitor center) through several specialty gardens on the return to the conservatory plaza. If time permits and the Day Chapel is open, hike a short distance to view this beautiful structure nestled in its wooded setting.

Miles and Directions

0.0 Descend from the conservatory plaza to the Shade Garden. GPS: N33 54.135' / W83 23.027'

0.6 Use the gate to follow the trail past the fenced area. GPS: N33 54.318' / W83 23.203'

1.3 Bear to the left at the outer boundary of the White Trail, and begin your return toward the river. GPS: N33 54.459' / W83 22.790'

2.4 Continue straight at the Red Trail intersection. A short distance ahead is a sheltered bench near the intersection of the Green Trail.

2.8 The White Trail bends left at the Middle Oconee River. GPS: N33 54.331' / W83 23.518'

3.4 Merge with the Orange Trail at a power-line corridor. GPS: N33 53.998' / W83 23.263'

3.9 The Orange Trail bends away from the river along the edge of a marsh.

4.6 Reach the trail's terminus at the parking area. It is 0.3 mile back to the conservatory plaza.

4.9 Arrive back at the trailhead.

Nearby Attractions

Historic Athens Welcome Center, 280 East Dougherty St., Athens 30601; (706) 353-1820; www.athenswelcomecenter.com

University of Georgia Visitor Center, Four Towers Building, 405 College Station Rd., Athens 30602; (706) 542-0842; www.visit.uga.edu

Sandy Creek Nature Center, 205 Old Commerce Rd., Athens 30607; (706) 613-3615; www.athensclarkecounty.com (includes information on the Oconee Rivers Greenway trails)

GREEN TIP
Recycle your old gear by giving it to someone
or an organization that will reuse it.

33 Stone Mountain Park: Cherokee Trail and Upper Walk-Up Trail

Rising nearly 800 feet above the piedmont hills and encompassing nearly 600 acres of exposed granite, 300-million-year-old Stone Mountain and the 3,200-acre park surrounding it have long been among Georgia's premier tourist destinations. While the mountain may be best known for the massive carving of Confederate leaders Jefferson Davis, Robert E. Lee, and Stonewall Jackson, the park offers lakes and golf courses, excursion trains and aerial trams, a re-created antebellum plantation, and Crossroads living history village. The hike described here follows the Cherokee Trail, which encircles the mountain and intersects with the Walk-Up Trail to the summit (a National Historic Trail).

Start: The Grist Mill parking area on the eastern side of the park

Distance: 5.5-mile loop (a round-trip to the summit on the Walk-Up Trail will add 1.8 miles)

Approximate hiking time: 3 to 4 hours

Elevation gain/loss: 358 feet; 824 feet if you hike to the summit

Trail surface: Compacted soil, bare rock

Lay of the land: Wooded hills, creek bottoms, and exposed rock slopes

Difficulty: Moderate to strenuous

Seasons: Year-round

Canine compatibility: Leashed dogs permitted on all trails except the Songbird Habitat Trail and the Walk-Up Trail

Land status: Stone Mountain Memorial Park Association

Fees and permits: Daily parking fee; annual pass available. Park attractions are individually priced or included in full attractions tickets.

Nearest town: Stone Mountain

Maps: USGS Stone Mountain and Snellville; maps also available from entrance stations and from the park website

Trail contact: Stone Mountain Park, US 78 East, Stone Mountain 30087; (770) 498-5690 or (800) 401-2407; www.stonemountainpark .com

Finding the trailhead: From the Atlanta perimeter (I-285), take US 78 (exit 39, Stone Mountain Freeway) and drive east for 12.5 miles to Stone Mountain Park (exit 8); bear right (south) on park entrance road. From the entrance station, drive west on Jefferson Davis Drive and bear left (south) on Robert E. Lee Boulevard. At approximately 3.5 miles, reach the Grist Mill parking area on the left. The hike begins below the parking area by the old mill. GPS: N33 48.331' / W84 08.119'

The Hike

From the Grist Mill parking area, follow the path down to the white-blazed Cherokee Trail (marked by a granite marker with a red park logo). Turn right along Stone Mountain Lake and across a narrow terrace banked by a stone wall before reaching

Cherokee Trail along face of mountain

the western side of a covered bridge (c. 1891, relocated to the park from Oconee County) at 0.3 mile. Continue straight, crossing two areas of exposed rock with views of the lake and bridge.

The Cherokee Trail reenters the woods and winds through a rocky area before climbing away from the water over several shallow ridges, reaching an intersection at 1.3 miles. The path to the right leads to Robert E. Lee Boulevard, and the trail ahead follows the northern bank of Venable Lake. Turn left and cross an earthen dam, bending right to follow the lake's southern shore.

Granite trail sign on Cherokee Trail

The trail crosses Stonewall Jackson Drive at 2.2 miles and reenters the woods near a small pond. From there, the path descends to a wetland before climbing on steps to another dam crossing. On the far side, follow the path to the right of a fenced playground, reaching an intersection with Lee Boulevard at 2.6 miles.

Reenter the woods by the granite trail sign, descending a short stairway to a level path through a hardwood forest. After an ascent toward the mountain, the trail passes a stone chimney (remnant of a long-vanished cabin) at 3.0 miles. From there, it bends right and descends past a connecting path to the Nature Gardens Trail before crossing

Only the hardiest plants can survive in the harsh and forbidding landscapes of granite outcrops like Stone Mountain. Among the best known is the Confederate daisy (*Helianthus porteri*), which thrives in the thin soils and shallow depressions on Stone Mountain and other nearby rock outcrops. First identified as a unique plant by Reverend Thomas Porter in 1846, the daisy is found only within a 60-mile radius of Stone Mountain. When the flower blooms in late August, the slopes of the mountain are carpeted with the small yellow flowers. Stone Mountain Park's Yellow Daisy Festival is held each year on the weekend after Labor Day and celebrates the beauty of this unique native flower.

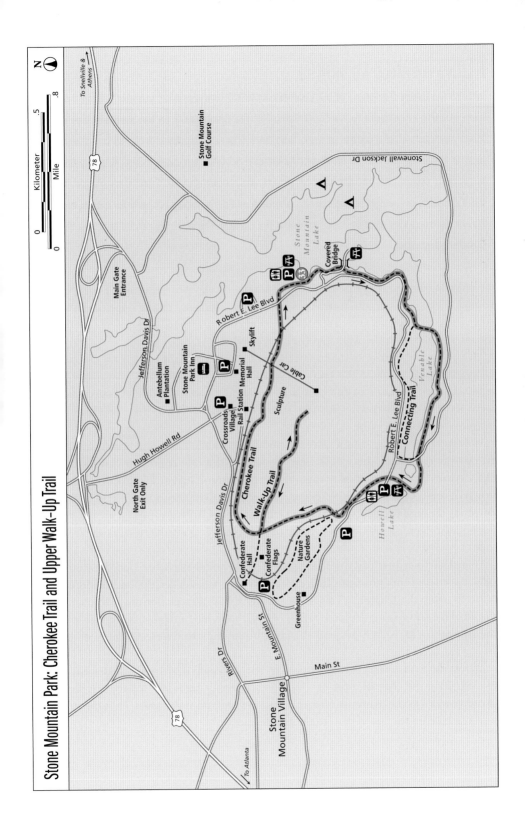

Stone Mountain Park: Cherokee Trail and Upper Walk-Up Trail

A LONG-AWAITED MEMORIAL

In 1915 the United Daughters of the Confederacy (UDC) commissioned sculptor Gutzon Borglum to carve a memorial to the "Lost Cause" of the Confederacy on the northern face of Stone Mountain. After a decade of work, Borglum left over a dispute with the UDC and went west to carve the presidents on Mount Rushmore. Sculptor Augustus Lukeman attempted to continue the project, but the lease on the mountain expired in 1928 and work ceased. In 1958 the state of Georgia purchased the mountain and surrounding property for a park, and Walker Hancock was commissioned to finish the carving. The work was completed and the sculpture dedicated in 1970.

the railroad tracks and climbing to Stone Mountain's exposed rock slope. Follow the white blazes painted on the rock as the trail winds diagonally up the slope to the left. After a strenuous climb, cross a service road and enter a wooded area before reaching the intersection with the Walk-Up Trail at 3.6 miles.

If you choose to hike to the top of the mountain, turn right and follow the steep, rocky path for 0.9 mile to the summit plaza at 4.5 miles. From there, you may enjoy a 360-degree panorama of the park and surrounding area, including a spectacular view of the Atlanta skyline to the west. Retrace your steps back to the Cherokee Trail intersection and turn right.

The path descends, at times steeply, through a wooded area and across the rock face before reentering the woods near the base of the mountain at 5.7 miles. Bear right at the intersection of an orange-blazed connecting trail, following the Cherokee Trail south of the railroad tracks and Crossroads living history village. The path descends through a creek valley before climbing to a large meadow (viewing area for popular evening laser shows) beneath the massive Confederate carving at 6.4 miles.

Cross the meadow, past a reflecting pool, and reenter the woods on the eastern side at a marked trail junction. Turn right on a service road, descending a short distance to rejoin the Cherokee Trail. Turn left and follow a creek bottom before crossing a bridge and passing a picnic area. The trail bears left and ascends steps to cross the railroad tracks. It then descends, bending to the right to intersect again with Lee Boulevard at 7.1 miles.

Cross the road and reenter the woods by the trail sign. Bear right and descend to the left along the edge of a picnic area. The trail bends right and follows a spillway carrying water to the gristmill. After reaching the old mill at 7.2 miles, cross the spillway and hike up the paved path to the parking area.

Miles and Directions

0.0 Begin the hike below the Grist Mill parking area. At the intersection with the white-blazed Cherokee Trail, turn right. GPS: N33 48.331' / W84 08.119'

0.3 Pass the old covered bridge and cross the road to the rock outcrop. GPS: N33 48.155' / W84 08.039'

1.3 At the Venable Lake Dam, turn left at the trail intersection. GPS: N33 47.863' / W84 08.347'

2.2 Cross Stonewall Jackson Drive and reenter the woods by the trail marker. GPS: N33 47.884' / W84 09.068'

2.6 Cross Robert E. Lee Boulevard by the playground and reenter the woods at the trail marker. GPS: N33 48.010' / W84 09.195'

3.1 Just past the railroad crossing, you reach the open rock face of the mountain. On the surface of the mountain, follow the painted white blazes. GPS: N33 48.282' / W84 09.361'

3.6 Turn right at the Walk-Up Trail. GPS: N33 48.580' / W 84 09.434'

4.5 After you reach the mountain summit, retrace your steps back to the Cherokee Trail. GPS: N33 48.367' / W84 08.760' at the summit

5.7 Bear right at the trail intersection near the base of the mountain. GPS: N33 48.721' / W84 09.302'

6.4 Cross the open meadow beneath the carving. GPS: N33 48.567' / W84 08.706'

7.1 Cross Robert E. Lee Boulevard. GPS: N33 48.484' / W84 08.179'

7.3 Return to the Grist Mill and your starting point.

34 Davidson-Arabia Mountain Nature Preserve

One of the most remarkable and unusual hikes in the Atlanta area, the trails across the exposed granite hills, wetlands, and pine/oak forests at Arabia Mountain take you back nearly a half-billion years in time. Arabia Mountain is a monadnock, an isolated outcrop of exposed rock, near Lithonia (Greek for "place of rock"). In 1973 the Davidson Mineral Company donated the property to DeKalb County for a park. In 2006 Arabia Mountain, Panola Mountain, and surrounding areas were recognized by the National Park Service as the Arabia Mountain National Heritage Area. In addition to park trails, a PATH Foundation multiuse trail links Arabia Mountain, Panola Mountain, and other local destinations.

Start: Davidson-Arabia Mountain Nature Preserve parking area

Distance: 7.4 miles of interconnected loops with linear connecting trail

Approximate hiking time: 3 to 4 hours

Elevation gain/loss: 172 feet

Trail surface: A mix of pavement, compacted soil, boardwalks, and exposed rock

Lay of the land: Large rock outcrops, woodlands, wetlands

Difficulty: Moderate due to distance and gentle climbs

Seasons: Best in spring and fall

Other trail users: PATH trail is open to bicyclists and inline skaters

Canine compatibility: Leashed dogs permitted

Land status: DeKalb County Parks and Recreation Department

Fees and permits: Free

Schedule: Open daily from sunrise to sunset

Nearest town: Lithonia

Maps: USGS Redan and Conyers; park maps also available at the nature center and on the Arabia Alliance website

Trail contact: Davidson-Arabia Mountain Nature Preserve, 3787 Klondike Rd., Lithonia 30038; 404-998-8384; www.arabiaalliance. org. The site also includes information about the PATH trail linking Arabia Mountain and Panola Mountain State Conservation Park.

Finding the trailhead: Travel east on I-20 to Evans Mill Road (exit 74). The exit ramp becomes Evans Mill Parkway. Turn at the second traffic light, at Evans Mill Road. Soon Evans Mill Road turns right, but keep straight onto Woodrow Drive. At 1.1 miles, Woodrow ends at Klondike Road. Turn right (south) and follow Klondike Road for 2.2 miles to the park entrance and nature center. There is a satellite parking area farther south on Klondike, just past the North Goddard Road intersection. GPS: N33 40.344' / W84 06.972'

The Hike

Follow the paved trail behind the nature center to the Arabia Mountain PATH Trail and turn right. Shortly, turn left on the Mile Rock Trail toward quarry sites and Arabia Lake. In 0.1 mile, reach open rock outcrops and follow stacked stone cairns

Arabia Mountain slopes from Klondike Spur

marking the path, passing an old quarry structure on the left. At 0.6 mile, pause to read the information tablet at the Old Frog Pond. Continue to more quarry ruins and turn right, reaching Arabia Lake at 1.0 mile.

Turn right on the Forest Trail as it follows the shoreline and woods before climbing away from the water on a series of switchbacks. At 1.6 miles, reach the intersection with the Mary Wade Trail. This 0.1-mile side path leads past a large boulder outcrop to the grave of pioneer settler Mary Wade, who died in 1888. Return to the main trail and continue toward the paved PATH trail intersection, returning to the nature center at 2.3 miles.

Arabia Mountain is composed primarily of migmatite, created by the combination of granite and gneiss under enormous heat and pressure. During the time of the supercontinent Pangea, the rock of Arabia Mountain was more than 10 miles underneath the surface of the earth.

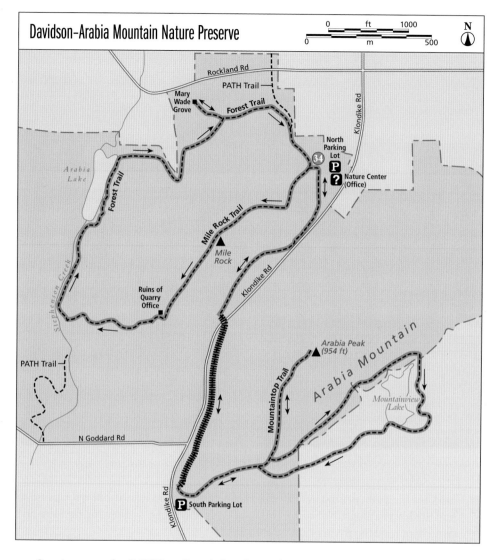

Davidson-Arabia Mountain Nature Preserve

Rockland Rd
PATH Trail
Mary Wade Grove
Forest Trail
Klondike Rd
North Parking Lot
34
P
Nature Center (Office)
Arabia Lake
Forest Trail
Mile Rock Trail
Mile Rock
Stephenson Creek
Ruins of Quarry Office
Klondike Rd
Arabia Peak (954 ft)
Arabia Mountain
PATH Trail
Mountaintop Trail
Mountainview Lake
N Goddard Rd
Klondike Rd
P South Parking Lot

Continue on the PATH trail as it bends southward to a spur trail that crosses Klondike Road at 2.8 miles. Across the road, turn right and follow the wooden boardwalk to the satellite parking area at 3.3 miles. A short distance east, past a pavilion, the Mountaintop Trail exits the woods and follows blazes and stacked-stone cairns on a northeasterly route toward the summit of Arabia Mountain. After a level walk, past the intersection with the Mountain View Trail, the path climbs to the mountain's summit at 3.9 miles.

After taking in the panoramic view, retrace your steps for 0.3 mile and turn left on the blue-blazed Mountain View Trail. The path meanders along the open rock face and through adjacent woods toward the eastern end of Mountain Lake. Follow the shoreline and bear right on an old road, crossing the dam at 5.7 miles.

Stone cairns on Arabia Mountain Summit Trail

ARABIA MOUNTAIN QUARRY SITES

Lithonia gneiss was long prized for its color, hardness, and ease of splitting. The first quarry opened on Arabia Mountain in 1879. The Arabia Mountain Stone Crushing Company was purchased by the Davidson family in 1895 and continued in operation (except for a brief period during the Depression) for more than eighty years. Stone from Arabia's quarries was used in buildings across the nation, including the US Military Academy at West Point, the Naval Academy at Annapolis, and—reportedly—for the Lincoln Memorial in Washington, DC. In 1973 the Davidson Granite Company donated Arabia Mountain to DeKalb County for use as a park, and quarry operations ceased in 1976. Today, old quarry sites, ponds, and buildings remain as reminders of the past.

Turn sharply left and descend before bearing right on switchbacks along the meadow, reaching the intersection with the Mountaintop Trail at 6.1 miles. Turn right and retrace your steps to the parking area, north along the boardwalk, and back to the nature center at 7.4 miles.

Miles and Directions

0.0 Begin hike behind the nature center parking area heading toward Arabia Lake on the Mile Rock Trail Peak. GPS: N33 40.344' / W84 06.972'

1.0 Arrive at Arabia Lake and the junction of the Forest Trail. Turn right onto the Forest Trail. GPS: N33 40.285' / W84 07.651'

1.9 Take a side trail to Mary Wade's grave.

2.8 Cross Klondike Road on a spur trail. GPS: N33 40.093' / W84 07.204'

3.9 Reach the summit of Arabia Mountain. GPS: N33 39.904' / W84 07.096'

5.7 Cross the Mountain Lake dam.

7.4 Return to the nature center.

35 Dauset Trails Nature Center

Created in 1977 by local business and civic leaders Hampton Daughtry and David Settle, Dauset Trails Nature Center is a 1,200-acre, private, nonprofit outdoor education and recreation area adjacent to Indian Springs State Park. The center offers more than 17 miles of hiking and mountain-biking trails and 10 miles of equestrian trails through a landscape of rolling hills, low ridges, and creek valleys. Dauset Trails also features a nature center and classroom building, picnic pavilions, group campground, and a lakeside chapel. The route described here is recommended by center staff as an introduction to the natural beauty of Dauset Trails.

Start: Trailhead parking area 0.1 mile west of Dauset Trails' main entrance on Mount Vernon Church Road

Distance: 5.8-mile circuit of interconnected loops

Approximate hiking time: 3 hours

Elevation gain/loss: 141 feet

Trail surface: Compacted soil and ground gravel

Lay of the land: Rolling piedmont hills, woodlands, wetlands

Difficulty: Moderate to difficult due to terrain and distance

Seasons: Year-round

Other trail users: Mountain bicyclists. (**Note:** While the trails do not close when wet, the nature center staff strongly urges bicyclists to refrain from riding in these conditions as this accelerates erosion.) In addition, a separate network of trails is dedicated to equestrian use.

Canine compatibility: Dogs allowed on leash (except in fenced nature center area)

Land status: Dauset Trails Nature Center

Fees and permits: Free (donations welcome)

Schedule: Trail hours are sunrise to 10 p.m., daily; nature center hours are 9 a.m. to 5 p.m. daily

Nearest town: Jackson

Maps: USGS Indian Springs; maps also available at the nature center and on the preserve website

Trail contact: Dauset Trails Nature Center, 360 Mount Vernon Church Rd., Jackson 30233; (770) 775-6798; www.dausettrails.com

Finding the trailhead: Drive south on I-75 to GA 36 (exit 201). Turn left (east), and cross the highway, driving 3.1 miles to High Falls Road. Turn right (south) and travel 2.4 miles to Mount Vernon Church Road and turn left (east). Follow Mount Vernon Church Road for 3.0 miles. Hikers are urged to park at the gravel entrance 0.1 mile west of the main entrance. The trailhead parking area remains open after the main gates are closed at 5 p.m. GPS: N33 13.966' / W83 56.988'

The Hike

(**Note:** Trails are marked by numbered signs at major intersections. Reference maps are available at the center and online.)

From the trailhead parking area, pass the information board and follow the service road to the intersection of the Bootlegger and Moonshine Trails. Turn right and follow the Moonshine Trail as it bends left above a deepening ravine, passing the group

Numbered blazes on nature center trails

campground at 0.5 mile. Descend past the chapel and picnic pavilion to the gravel road and turn right. Cross the bridge over the pond's edge and turn right, following the path along the water before reentering the woods at 0.7 mile. Bear right, cross a bridge, and turn right along the path as it ascends away from the water. Pass another short bridge on the right that links to the Turkey Trot Trail and continue straight to signpost #14.

Follow the Turkey Trot Trail as it ascends to the Wagon Track Trail at 1.3 miles, near the entrance to an animal enclosure by the nature center. Turn left on the Wagon Track Trail and descend through a piedmont mixed forest. At the next trail inter-section, follow the hiker symbol (not the bike symbol) and continue to the creek bottom. Turn left, then right, across a footbridge by signpost #13. Bear sharply right, following the stream for a short distance before bearing left and ascending to an intersection with a gravel road at 1.7 miles.

Cross the road and reenter the woods on the Wagon Track Trail as it descends to a footbridge over an intermittent stream, reaching a creek bottom at 2.1 miles. At the intersection, turn right on the Pine Mountain Trail (the "wrong way" sign is for bikers) and follow the meandering stream, crossing a shallow ridge and rock outcrops, before turning away from the water near signpost #17 at 2.6 miles.

The path ascends by switchbacks over several ridges, bearing left at a trail fork and then bending sharply left as it crosses a dry creek bed at 3.0 miles. A short distance ahead, the path skirts the edge of a small meadow and climbs to an intersection with the gravel road at 3.3 miles (signpost #16).

Turn right, following the gravel road past the previous intersection with the Wagon Track Trail on a descent to the pond. Retrace your steps past the water and ascend toward the picnic area at 3.7 miles. Turn right, cross a small meadow, and

Small stream along path near Turkey Trot Trail

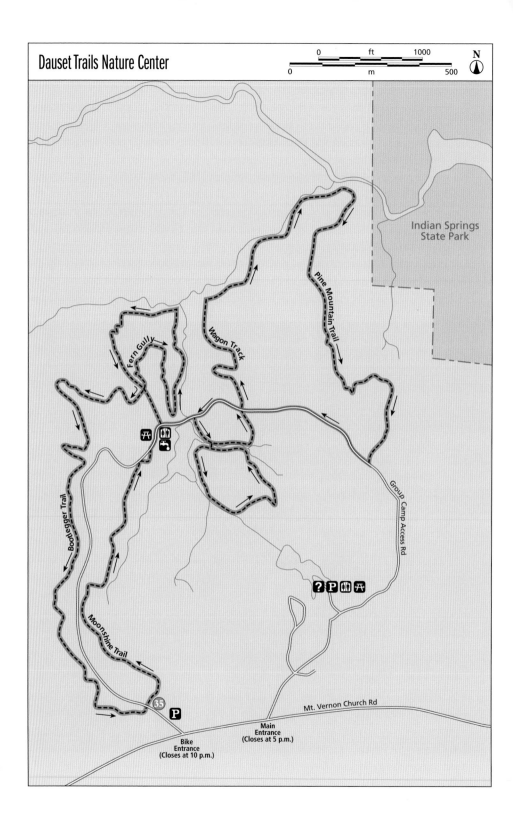

0   ft   1000

0   m   500

N

Indian Springs
State Park

Pine Mountain Trail

Wagon Track

Fern Gully

Bootlegger Trail

Group Camp Access Rd

Moonshine Trail

35

P

? **P**

Mt. Vernon Church Rd

Main
Entrance
(Closes at 5 p.m.)

Bike
Entrance
(Closes at 10 p.m.)

reenter the woods on the Wagon Track Trail (sign #18). Hike to a four-way trail intersection and turn right on the Fern Gully Trail, descending on long switchbacks to a wetlands area of ferns and grasses.

Continue to a trail intersection by a suspension bridge across an intermittent stream at 4.4 miles. Turn left, away from the bridge, and follow the creek for about 0.1 mile before bending away from the water on a moderate ascent. After crossing several ridges, return to the four-way intersection at 4.7 miles.

Turn right onto the Bootlegger Trail and climb to a meadow, following the right-hand edge before reentering the woods. Turn sharply left and cross another small meadow. The path levels out and follows the preserve boundary line, meandering over rolling terrain before reaching the gravel service road and the end of the Bootlegger Trail at 5.8 miles (sign #20). The parking area is a short distance away to the right.

Miles and Directions

0.0 From the trailhead parking area, pass the information board and follow the service road. Turn right on Moonshine Trail. GPS: N33 13.966' / W83 56.988'

0.5 Pass a group camp, chapel, and picnic pavilion. GPS: N33 14.288' / W83 57.049'

0.7 Cross the pond spillway and follow the path to the right along the edge of the pond.

1.3 Turn left onto the Wagon Track Trail by the gated enclosure. GPS: N33 14.300' / W83 56.748'

1.7 Cross the gravel road and reenter the woods. GPS: N33 14.463' / W83 56.848'

2.1 Reach the creek bottom and turn right on the Pine Mountain Trail. GPS: N33 14.637' / W83 56.909'

3.3 Turn right on the gravel road at signpost #16, the terminus of the Pine Mountain Trail. GPS: N33 14.372' / W83 56.586'

3.7 Cross the meadow by the picnic shelters and reenter the woods on the Wagon Track Trail. GPS: N33 14.462' / W83 56.980'

4.4 Bear left before crossing the footbridge over the creek.

4.7 Return to the four-way intersection and turn right on Bootlegger Trail.

5.8 Reach the service road at the end of the Bootlegger Trail. The parking area is a short distance ahead on the right.

HEALING MINERAL SPRINGS

Nearby Indian Springs State Park preserves mineral springs that Native Americans believed had healing properties. A condition of the 1825 Treaty of Indian Springs (between the Creeks and the state of Georgia) was that the springs would remain open to the public in perpetuity. This is the basis for the claim that Indian Springs was the nation's "first" state park. Much of the current park was built during the 1930s by the Civilian Conservation Corps (CCC).

36 Cochran Mill Park

Following cession of Creek lands in Georgia in 1826, Cheadle Cochran received this property as reward for service in the War of 1812 and built a gristmill on Little Bear Creek. In 1870 Cheadle's elder son, Berry, erected a mill on nearby Bear Creek, later converting the dam for hydroelectric power for the town of Palmetto. Acquired by Fulton County in the 1970s, the 800-acre park was purchased by the city of Chattahoochee Hills in 2010. Through a 2013 Recreation Trails Program grant from the Georgia Department of Natural Resources, the park's trail system was greatly expanded for use by hikers, bikers, and equestrians. In 2016, the Cochran Mill Nature Center, a private facility within the park, closed permanently.

Start: Cochran Mill Park parking area on Cochran Mill Road
Distance: 8.5 miles of interconnected loops linked by a linear trail, and a lollipop to Henry Mill Falls
Approximate hiking time: 4 hours
Difficulty: Moderate due to distance and rolling terrain
Elevation gain/loss: 202 feet
Trail surface: Mix of compacted dirt and exposed rock
Lay of the land: Upland forest, bogs, and lowland forests
Seasons: Year-round
Canine compatibility: Leashed dogs permitted
Land status: City of Chattahoochee Hills Parks and Recreation Department

Fees and permits: Daily parking fee; annual pass available (residents of Chattahoochee Hills admitted free with city-issued parking pass)
Schedule: Open daily
Nearest town: Chattahoochee Hills
Maps: USGS Palmetto; trail maps also available at pay station kiosk or online at www.chatthillsga.us/departments/parks-recreation
Trail contacts: City of Chattahoochee Hills Parks and Recreation Department, 6505 Rico Rd., Chattahoochee Hills, GA 30268; (770) 463-8881; www.chatthillsga.us/departments/parks-recreation

Finding the trailhead: Drive south on I-85 to Old National Highway/South Fulton Parkway (exit 69). Bear right (west) and continue on South Fulton Parkway for 16 miles to Cochran Mill Road. Turn right (north) and travel 0.5 mile to the park entrance on the left, at 6875 Cochran Mill Rd. The parking area includes picnic pavilions, a playground, and a comfort station. GPS: N33 34.281' / W84 42.792'

The Hike

From the parking area, cross Cochran Mill Road and follow the Orange Trail (an old gravel road) a short distance toward Bear Creek. Before reaching the closed bridge, bear left and follow the trail along the western side of the creek. At 0.4 mile, the

Bear Creek Trail in winter

Henry Mill Falls on Bear Creek

trail returns to the road and crosses a bridge (watch for traffic) before reentering the woods on the right. Continue straight past an intersection and reach the open field and picnic area below Cochran Mill Falls at 0.8 mile.

From the east side of the meadow, ascend on the orange-blazed Cochran Mill Loop Trail as it follows a streambed. Continue on the trail's outer loop eastward along the wooded slope before descending to the banks of Bear Creek at 2.0 miles. Turn left, noting the ruins of Berry Cochran's mill and dam to your right. The orange trail ascends the slope, continuing past a footbridge across the creek at 2.6 miles (the bridge connects with trails of the closed nature center). Continue straight, closing the loop and turning right on the orange trail to return to Cochran Mill Road. Turn right and follow the road, crossing a bridge, to a pedestrian crossing sign at 2.8 miles. Turn left and reenter the woods on the multiuse, red-blazed Turnpike Trail.

The trail follows rolling terrain and passes through a lowland area before ascending to an intersection at 3.3 miles. Continue straight on the red-blazed Big Ridge Loop Trail, which heads over a ridge and across a stream as it climbs away on a series of long switchbacks. The path follows the slope's contours before descending past a rock outcrop and boulder field to the intersection with the Bear Creek Trail at 5.4 miles.

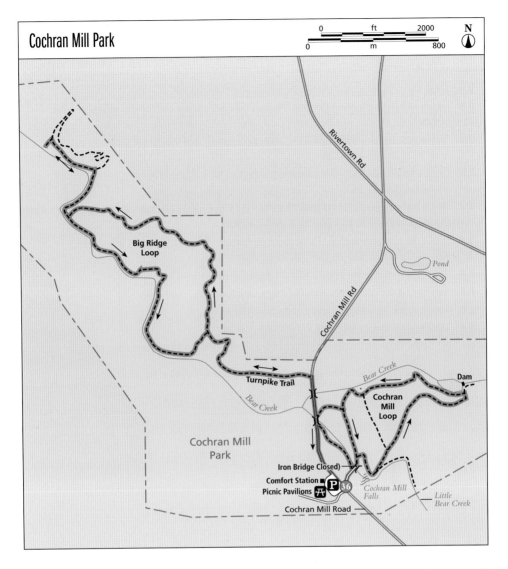

Cochran Mill Park

0 ft 2000
0 m 800
N

Rivertown Rd

Pond

Cochran Mill Rd

Big Ridge
Loop

Turnpike Trail

Bear Creek

Bear Creek

Dam

Cochran
Mill
Loop

Cochran Mill
Park

Iron Bridge Closed)
Comfort Station
Picnic Pavilions
P 36

Cochran Mill
Falls

Little
Bear Creek

Cochran Mill Road

Turn right, crossing a wetland and over a bridge on the red-blazed 5 Turn Hill Trail. The red trail ascends to the right, but you continue straight, following Bear Creek on an unmarked path. At 5.7 miles, a short walk left leads to open rocks and a panoramic view of Henry Mill Falls.

Retrace your steps past the Big Ridge Loop Trail, and continue straight on the Bear Creek Trail as it follows the water. Soon, you will climb away from the creek, then descend again on switchbacks to a footbridge across a stream. The path bends left, passing through a wetland area, before climbing away from the water to reconnect with the Big Ridge Loop Trail at 7.5 miles. Retrace your steps to Cochran Mill Road and turn right. Follow the road's shoulder to reach the parking area at 8.5 miles.

Miles and Directions

0.0 Begin hiking at the Cochran Mill Park parking area. Cross the road on the orange-blazed Cochran Mill Trail. GPS: N33 34.281' / W84 42.792'

0.4 Cross the road bridge and reenter the woods on the orange trail.

0.8 Reach an open area below Cochran Mill Falls. Turn left and ascend the orange trail into the woods.

2.0 Turn left on the loop trail above Bear Creek. Note the ruins of the old mill and dam. GPS: N33 34.563' / W84 42.328'

2.8 Cross Cochran Mill Road and reenter the woods on the red-blazed Turnpike Trail. GPS: N33 34.613' / W84 42.897'

3.3 Reach the intersection of the Bear Creek and Big Ridge Loop Trails. Continue straight on Big Ridge Loop. GPS: N33 34.730' / W84 43.295'

5.4 Reach the intersection of Big Ridge and Bear Creek Trails. Turn right on the red-blazed 5 Turn Hill Trail. GPS: N33 35.152' / W84 43.757'

5.4 Reach the rock outcrop below Henry Mill Falls. GPS: N33 35.333' / W84 43.871'

7.5 Turn right at the intersection onto Big Ridge Loop Trail.

8.0 Turn right and follow the shoulder of Cochran Mill Road.

8.5 Arrive back at the parking area.

37 McIntosh Reserve

Few sites in the piedmont hills surrounding Atlanta surpass the scenic beauty and historical significance of the 527-acre McIntosh Reserve. The park was once the home of William McIntosh, a Creek chief and veteran of the War of 1812. In 1825 McIntosh was assassinated here by Creeks angered by his signing the Treaty of Indian Springs, ceding Creek lands in Georgia (his grave is across the road from the site of his home). In the early 1900s, Georgia Power purchased the land, planning to dam the Chattahoochee for hydroelectric power. The dam was never built, and in 1978 the company donated the property to Carroll County for a park.

Start: Parking area by comfort station and old ranger office
Distance: 6.9-mile circuit of interconnected loops
Approximate hiking time: 4 hours
Elevation gain/loss: 300 feet
Trail surface: Sandy floodplain, packed dirt, gravel
Lay of the land: River floodplain, wetlands, wooded upland slopes, meadows, and recreation fields
Difficulty: Moderate to difficult based on distance and terrain
Seasons: Year-round

Other trail users: Equestrians
Canine compatibility: Leashed dogs permitted
Land status: Carroll County Parks and Recreation
Fees and permits: Daily parking fee
Schedule: Open daily from 8 a.m. to 8 p.m. spring, summer, and fall; 8 a.m. to 7 p.m. in winter
Nearest town: Whitesburg
Maps: USGS Whitesburg; trail maps available at the nature center
Trail contact: McIntosh Reserve, 1046 West McIntosh Circle, Whitesburg 30185; (770) 830-5879; www.carrollcountyga.com

Finding the trailhead: Travel south on I-85 to GA 34 (exit 47). At the exit turn right (north) and drive a short distance to West Bypass 34. Turn right and drive 4.5 miles to GA 16/North Alternate US 27. Turn right (north) again, and travel 8.5 miles to Whitesburg. At the traffic circle, turn left (west) and travel 1.5 miles to West McIntosh Circle (watch for a small road sign). Turn left (south) and drive about a mile to the entrance station. After checking in, travel another 0.5 mile to a parking area above the river near the old ranger station. GPS: N33 26.537' / W84 57.108'

The Hike

Cross the road from the parking area, hiking past an outdoor classroom and picnic area to an observation platform overlooking the Chattahoochee River. Descend through the picnic area and campground to the River Trail, which follows the floodplain toward the west. After crossing a footbridge over a stream, reach the rocky outcrop known as "Council Bluffs" at 0.6 mile.

Bear left at a trail fork, remaining on the River Trail as it winds along the water. To your right is a large recreation field used for a variety of events and activities. At

Re-creation of McIntosh House

1.5 miles, the trail bends right, away from the water, and curves east, following the meadow's edge for another 0.5 mile.

After bending sharply left, the Beaver Pond Trail turns right and enters the woods on a shallow ascent across a ridge. You will descend along the edge of a wetland area. The trail climbs another ridge, reaching an intersection at 2.4 miles. Turn right on the Cedar Bluff Trail and continue climbing toward the horse-trailer parking area, where you will turn left.

A short distance ahead, cross the edge of the parking lot and reenter the woods on the Cedar Bluff Trail, a gentle ascent that parallels the park road. After crossing a ridge at 2.8 miles, the trail descends to a narrow ravine and climbs the far slope, passing the park's maintenance area. Ahead, you will bend to the right, descending to a stream crossing before climbing a moderate slope and passing near the park's check-in station. The trail merges with a gated gravel service road at 3.3 miles. Continue on the gravel road for about a hundred yards before the Outer Boundary Trail exits to the left.

Follow the occasionally rutted Outer Boundary Trail as it descends to a creek bottom, where the path bends right and ascends a moderate slope. The trail continues along a series of gentle switchbacks, reaching another gravel road at 3.9 miles. Cross and descend a short distance before following a meandering path crossing several shallow streams surrounded by a carpet of ferns.

THE SCOTTISH CREEK CHIEF

A Creek chief named "McIntosh" may seem strange. William McIntosh was actually the grandson of John McIntosh, a Scot who sailed to Georgia in 1733 with the colony's founder, General James Oglethorpe. His son, William, was a loyalist during the Revolution who recruited Creeks to fight for England. During his time in Georgia's interior, he married Senoia, a princess of the Wind Clan of the Lower Creek Nation. Their son, William Jr., grew to become chief of the Coweta Town, located on the Chattahoochee near present-day Columbus. McIntosh sought to bridge the divide between his people and the settlers, choosing to ally with the Americans during the War of 1812, fighting alongside General Andrew Jackson at the Battle of Horseshoe Bend in Alabama. Ironically, President Jackson urged removal of the natives from Georgia and was supported in this by the state's governor, George Troup—who was William McIntosh's cousin.

In 1821 McIntosh held a council at the Reserve of Cherokee and Creek leaders to establish boundaries between the two nations (roughly the Chattahoochee River, with Creek lands south of the river and Cherokee lands to the north) and to seek mutual support against further Euro-American settlement. A large rock outcrop on the banks of the river, long called "Council Bluffs," is believed to have been the site of this gathering.

Historic Council Bluffs

Trail along floodplain near Council Bluffs

At 4.2 miles, cross the park entrance road and follow the contours of several shallow ridges on a gentle descent. The path reaches the site of an abandoned group camping area at 4.7 miles. Turn right, then quickly left, on the Moonshiner's Alley Trail as it climbs to a ridge. As you walk, you will see evidence of a fire that scorched many of the surrounding woodlands.

After descending, the trail bends sharply left at an intersection (the path straight ahead leads to the check-in station) and meanders through a lowland area. Cross on stones over a streambed before bending left across another creek on a footbridge. The

McIntosh Reserve

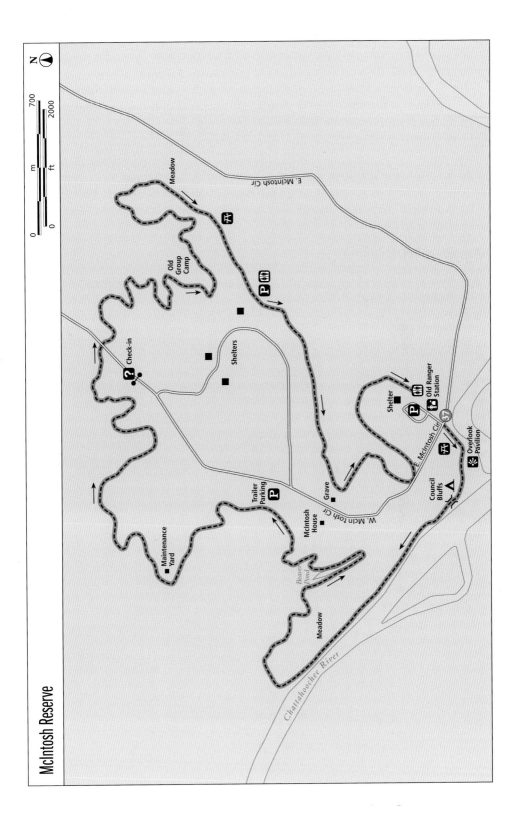

path bends sharply right and exits the woods to a recreation field. Bear right and hike past a group picnic shelter, small ponds, a playground, and a comfort station.

The Moonshiner's Alley Trail reenters the woods to the left of a paved road, bending to the right on a gentle ascent to the edge of a meadow at 6.1 miles. Nearby are Chief McIntosh's grave and the 180-year-old cabin that sits on the site of his home. The trail reenters the woods across the meadow from the grave site, descending above a deep ravine.

At 6.5 miles, the trail joins the road to cross a bridge, reentering the woods to the left on the far side. Climb to a ridgetop intersection with the Eagle's Nest Trail (a 1.1-mile loop). Turn right instead, and descend a short distance to your starting point at 6.9 miles.

Miles and Directions

0.0 Begin at the gravel parking area by the old ranger station. GPS: N33 26.537' / W84 57.108'

0.6 After crossing a footbridge on the River Trail, reach the Council Bluffs. GPS: N33 26.498' / W84 57.361'

1.5 Bear right at the end of the River Trail onto the Beaver Pond Trail. GPS: N33 26.964' / W84 57.971'

2.4 Bear left at the trail intersection below the horse-trailer parking area. GPS: N33 26.810' / W84 57.443'

3.3 Merge with the gravel service road. GPS: N33 27.230' / W84 57.222'

4.2 Cross the park entrance road on the Outer Boundary Trail. GPS: N33 27.386' / W84 56.952'

5.6 At the edge of the open field, bear right on the dirt road to the group shelter. GPS: N33 26.952' / W84 56.994'

6.1 Bear left and pause at Chief McIntosh's grave and home site. GPS: N33 26.743' / W84 57.365'

6.9 Return to the parking area.

Honorable Mentions

I. Chastain Park PATH Trail, Lake Forrest and Wieuca Roads, Atlanta 30342; PATH Foundation: (404) 875-7284; https://pathfoundation.org/trails/chastain-park

Part of the PATH network of trails in the Atlanta area, this popular path draws thousands of visitors who walk or jog on double loop trails that are marked as 5K (3.1-mile), and a separate 3K loop. The combined paved and dirt trails border an eighteen-hole golf course, tennis center, and public park with recreation fields and playground. Also nearby is the Chastain Park Amphitheater.

J. Chattahoochee Nature Center Trails, 9135 Willeo Rd., Roswell 30075; (770) 992-2055; www.chattnaturecenter.org

Established in 1976 as a nonprofit educational organization, the Chattahoochee Nature Center (CNC) is located on 127 acres along the northern banks of the Chattahoochee River, south of Roswell. The CNC features classrooms, exhibit spaces, and more than 2.5 miles of trails meandering through wetlands, past ponds, and into upland hills. The center offers a wide variety of school programs, as well as outdoor educational and recreational programs for the entire community. The wetland trails along the river are an excellent location for observing waterfowl. The trails are easy to moderate in difficulty with some steep hills.

The center may be reached by traveling north on GA 400 to Northridge Road (exit 6). Bear right (west) and cross the highway bridge and turn right (north) on Dunwoody Place. Drive 1.2 miles to the intersection with Roswell Road and turn right (north). Travel 1.1 miles, across the Chattahoochee River bridge, and turn left (west) at the traffic light on Azalea Drive. Follow Azalea for 1.5 miles, past Fulton County's Chattahoochee River Park, to Willeo Road. Turn left (south) on Willeo. Drive 0.5 mile, and the center's entrance is on the right.

K. Silver Comet Trail: Florence Road to Dallas

The next western-leading section of the Silver Comet Trail, past Florence Road, traces an 8-mile point-to-point route through an increasingly rural landscape as Atlanta recedes in the distance. Highlights along this portion of the trail include a bridge over the Norfolk-Southern Railroad tracks (a popular stop for train buffs) near milepost 15, and a climb to the highest point on the Silver Comet Trail (1,100 feet above sea level) between mileposts 18 and 19. In addition, there are interesting shops and eateries in Hiram and Dallas. The path is easy to moderate due to distance and gentle grades.

To reach Dallas from Florence Road, drive west on US 278 for 8.4 miles, crossing GA 92 and GA 120, before reaching GA 61. Turn left (south) and park at the trail access area by the Paulding Chamber of Commerce.

L. Tribble Mill Park, 2125 Tribble Mill Pkwy., Lawrenceville 30045; (770) 978-5270; www.gwinnetcounty.com

Surrounding the site of the now-vanished nineteenth-century Tribble Mill (inundated by the waters of the park's lakes), 700-acre Tribble Mill Park is one of Gwinnett County's premier recreation destinations. The park features a large playground for children; an outdoor amphitheater; fishing and boating on 108-acre Ozora Lake and on 40-acre Chandler Lake; and more than 12 miles of multiuse trails for hikers, bikers, and equestrians. Especially popular is the 3.4-mile paved path around Ozora Lake. The trail difficulty is easy on the paved trail due to the surface and gentle grades. The dirt trails are easy to moderate based on length and elevation changes.

To reach the park from Atlanta, travel I-285 to Stone Mountain Freeway/US 78 (exit 39-B). Drive east on US 78, through Snellville, for 16.3 miles to Grayson Parkway/GA 84 and turn left (north). Drive 5.6 miles (the road name changes to Grayson–New Hope Road) and turn right (east) on Tribble Mill Parkway. You will find parking areas throughout the park.

M. Dauset Trails Nature Center: Backcountry Multiuse Trails

Beyond the trails profiled in the Dauset Trails chapter, the preserve offers an additional 10 miles of backcountry trails for hiking and mountain biking, as well as a separate 10-mile network of trails for equestrian use. Dauset Trails is a destination to explore many times and over all the seasons. The trails vary in difficulty from easy to moderate based on distance and terrain.

N. Charlie Elliott Wildlife Center Multiuse Trail, Marben Farm Road, Mansfield 30055; (770) 784-3059; www.georgia wildlife.com/charlieelliott

Open to hikers, bicyclists, and equestrians, the path traces a 5.6-mile loop through piedmont woods and creek bottoms a short distance west of the wildlife center's main trail network. All trail users must complete a free trail permit at the trailhead before entering. The trail may be closed during archery and turkey hunting seasons. Check with the wildlife center for trail closure information. To reach the trail from GA 11, turn left (east) on Marben Farm Road and travel 0.3 mile. The multiuse trail parking area is on the right.

O. Thompson Mills Forest and State Arboretum, 1898 New Liberty Church Rd., Braselton 30517; (706) 433-8713; www.warnell.uga.edu/ thompson-mills-forest-state-arboretum

This 333-acre property was donated to the University of Georgia's Warnell School of Forest Resources in 1980 and named the state's official arboretum in 1991. The grounds, used for research and teaching, as well as for public enjoyment, feature more than 7 miles of trails and unpaved roads leading through a pinetum, a native tree forest, and the Eva Thompson Thornton Memorial Garden. To reach the arboretum, travel north on I-85 to GA 211 (exit 126). Drive north, past Chateau Elan Winery and Resort, for 1.3 miles. Turn right on Liberty Church Road (which becomes Thompson Mill Road), and drive 1.4 miles to the entrance on New Liberty Church Road.

Appendix A:
Land Use Management Agencies and Organizations

Chattahoochee–Oconee National Forest

1755 Cleveland Hwy., Gainesville 30501; (770) 297-3000; www.fs.usda.gov/attmain/conf

The national forest website offers information on more than 430 miles of hiking trails in the Chattahoochee National Forest, which covers a large portion of the north Georgia mountains. Popular trails include the Appalachian National Scenic Trail, the Benton MacKaye Trail, and the Bartram Trail, as well as a path to Brasstown Bald, Georgia's highest point (4,484 feet above sea level). The national forest also has several natural areas, campgrounds, trout streams, and waterfalls.

The Oconee National Forest, located in the lower piedmont area southeast of Atlanta, has very limited hiking but offers fishing and recreational boating on local streams and lakes.

National Park Service

Southeast Regional Office, 100 Alabama St. SW, 1924 Building, Atlanta 30303; (404) 507-5600; www.nps.gov

Established in 1916 to oversee the nation's parklands, the agency now manages 391 units in forty-nine states, the District of Columbia, and several territories. Georgia hosts ten national park properties, from Chickamauga-Chattanooga National Military Park in the northwest corner of the state to Cumberland Island National Seashore on the southeastern coast. Park service trails profiled in *Best Hikes Atlanta* include three hikes at Kennesaw Mountain National Battlefield Park (www.nps.gov/kemo) and paths within eight units of the Chattahoochee River National Recreation Area (www.nps.gov/chat).

US Fish and Wildlife Service

www.fws.gov/refuges

President Theodore Roosevelt created the first national wildlife refuge at Pelican Island, Florida, in 1903, and the fish and wildlife service now manages nearly 550 refuges in fifty states. There are nine refuges in Georgia, including the Okefenokee Swamp in southeastern Georgia. Trails within the Piedmont National Wildlife Refuge (www.fws.gov/piedmont/) south of Atlanta are profiled in this guidebook.

US Army Corps of Engineers

Lake Allatoona: www.sam.usace.army.mil/Missions/Civil-Works/Recreation/Allatoona-Lake; Lake Sidney Lanier: www.sam.usace.army.mil/Missions/Civil-Works/Recreation/Lake-Sidney-Lanier

Lakes Allatoona and Sidney Lanier are two of the major corps of engineers' lakes in northern Georgia. The lakes, constructed for water resources and hydroelectric power, also offer fishing, recreational boating, camping, and picnicking resources. Laurel Ridge Trail near Lanier's Buford Dam is managed by the corps.

Georgia Department of Natural Resources

2 Martin Luther King Jr. Dr. SE, Suite 1252 East Tower, Atlanta 30334; (404) 656-3500; www.gadnr.org

The state's primary land management agency is responsible for a number of public land holdings across Georgia, including wildlife management areas, public fishing areas, and Georgia's state parks and historic sites. The agency also regulates hunting and fishing and oversees the Environmental Protection Division. Georgia DNR manages the Charlie Elliott Wildlife Center, which is profiled in this guide.

Georgia State Parks and Historic Sites

2600 GA 155, Stockbridge, GA 30281; (770) 389-7286; www.gastateparks.org

Considered among the best state parks agencies in the nation, Georgia's state parks agency operates forty-seven state parks, sixteen historic sites, and one excursion train. Trails in three state parks and one state historic site are profiled in this guide.

PATH Foundation

PO Box 14327, Atlanta 30324; (404) 875-7284; www.pathfoundation.org

This private, nonprofit organization has been instrumental in forming partnerships with public agencies to create and improve pedestrian pathways across the Atlanta area. PATH trails link downtown Atlanta and the Martin Luther King Jr. Historic District with the Carter Presidential Center and beyond, to Stone Mountain Park. Another PATH trail circles North Fulton Park's golf course, while a third meanders through Davidson-Arabia Mountain Heritage Preserve. PATH has also facilitated collaboration among public agencies and private supporters to develop the increasingly popular Silver Comet Trail, which links Atlanta to Alabama's Chief Ladiga Trail. Now the Atlanta BeltLine, a system of trails that will eventually encircle the city, is part of PATH. Two sections of the Silver Comet Trail and the BeltLine Eastside Trail are profiled in this guide.

Appendix B:
Outdoor Recreation and Environmental Protection Groups and Organizations

Atlanta Outdoor Club

PO Box 767335, Roswell, GA 30076; www.atlantaoutdoorclub.com

Founded in 2000, the club is an outdoor-oriented social organization for active adults of all ages. The club offers a variety of recreational events, from day hikes and backpacking trips to rafting journeys and destination weekends across the Atlanta area, Georgia, and the Southeast. There are no membership dues, and events are fee-based and require a reservation.

Georgia Walkers

1496 Elizabeth Ln., East Point, GA 30144; http://georgiawalkers.homestead.com

This membership organization is affiliated with the American Volksport Association (www.ava.org) and sponsors several Volksport (6.2-mile noncompetitive walks along defined routes) events each year, in addition to club outings to various destinations around Atlanta and the state.

Mosaic Jewish Outdoor Club of Georgia

www.meetup.com/Mosaic-Jewish-Outdoor-Club-of-Georgia

This group, associated with Mosaic Outdoor Clubs of America (www.mosaic outdoor.org), offers group outings, social events, and activities for Jewish adults and families.

Wilderness Network of Georgia

PO Box 79131, Atlanta, GA 30357-7131; www.meetup.com/wildnetga

Wilderness Network is a membership organization that serves the gay community in Atlanta and across the state. The group sponsors social gatherings and offers a wide variety of hikes and trips within Georgia and around the nation.

Women's Outdoor Network (WON)

(770) 937-6770; www.meetup.com/wonatlanta

A membership organization, WON provides group outdoor recreational opportunities for women eighteen and older. The organization hosts events nearly every weekend of the year. Outings may include hikes, backpacking treks, raft and canoe trips, and other activities.

Outdoor Outfitters

REI

www.rei.com

Local retail store locations are in Atlanta off I-85 North, near Perimeter Mall, in Buford near the Mall of Georgia, and on Barrett Parkway in Kennesaw. This Seattle, Washington-based retail chain offers everything you need for hiking, climbing, camping, biking, canoeing, and more. Each store features outdoor educational programs and classes, local events, and staff expertise to get you on your way to outdoor adventures.

High Country Outfitters

www.highcountryoutfitters.com

With locations in Atlanta, Buckhead, Sandy Springs, East Cobb, and Athens, High Country has been serving Atlanta's outdoor enthusiasts for more than thirty years. The stores carry and recommend equipment for hiking, backpacking, climbing, mountaineering, and paddling. The knowledgeable staff offers guidance on treks down the Chattahoochee or across the Patagonian wilderness. The store also hosts a wide variety of educational and instructional programs and group outings.

Dick's Sporting Goods

www.dickssportinggoods.com

This retail store has multiple locations in the Atlanta area. As a modern version of the old-fashioned sporting goods store, Dick's offers equipment for outdoor activities from hiking, biking, camping, and paddling to team sports of every kind.

Bass Pro Shops

5900 Sugarloaf Pkwy., Lawrenceville, GA 30043; (678) 847-5500; www.basspro.com

While the primary emphasis of this national chain is fishing and boating, stores offer a wide assortment of hiking apparel and camping equipment.

Cabela's

152 Northpoint Pkwy., Acworth, GA 30102; (470) 315-7500; www.cabelas.com

This chain of sporting goods stores has locations in the United States and Canada. Cabela's provides equipment for a wide range of outdoor activities.

Appendix C: Additional Resources

Benyus, Janine M. *The Field Guide to Wildlife Habitats of the Eastern United States.* New York: Fireside Books, 1989.

Brown, Fred, and Nell Jones, editors. *Highroad Guide to the Georgia Mountains.* Atlanta: Longstreet Press, 1999.

Davis, Ren and Helen. *Atlanta Walks: A Comprehensive Guide to Walking, Running, and Bicycling the Area's Scenic and Historic Locales.* 4th ed. Atlanta: Peachtree Publishers, 2011.

Davis, Ren and Helen. *Georgia Walks: Discovery Hikes through the Peach State's Natural and Human History.* Atlanta: Peachtree Publishers, 2001.

Golden, Randy and Pam. *60 Hikes within 60 Miles: Atlanta.* 3rd ed. Birmingham, AL: Menasha Ridge Press, 2013.

Homan, Tim. *The Hiking Trails of North Georgia.* 3rd ed. Atlanta: Peachtree Publishers, 1999.

McDonald, Jonah. *Hiking Atlanta's Hidden Forests: Intown and Out.* Almond, NC: Milestone Press, 2014.

Miles, Jim. *Fields of Glory: A History and Tour Guide of the Atlanta Campaign.* Nashville, TN: Rutledge Hill Press, 1989.

Pfitzer, Donald and Jimmy Jacobs. *Hiking Georgia: A Guide to Georgia's Greatest Hiking Adventures.* 4th ed. Guilford, CT: FalconGuides, 2014.

Wilson, Jim. *Common Birds of Greater Atlanta.* Athens: University of Georgia Press, 2011.

Online Resources

www.atlantatrails.com
A continually evolving website that features many popular walks, runs, and hikes in Atlanta and beyond.

www.georgiaencyclopedia.org
The *New Georgia Encyclopedia* is an ever-expanding resource to Georgia history, geology, archaeology, etc. Developed by the Georgia Humanities Council.

www.georgiatrails.com
A resource for hiking, biking, and driving destinations around Georgia.

www.rootsrated.com
A resource for hikes across the nation; includes a selection of popular Atlanta-area trails.

Hike Index

Tree canopy above Cochran Shoals Trail

About the Authors

Ren Davis is a native Atlantan with a lifelong interest in the city's and region's history. He earned a B.A. in American History from Emory University in 1973 and a master's degree in Healthcare Administration from Tulane University in 1976. He retired in 2009 from a career in administration at Crawford Long Hospital and Emory Healthcare. An avid hiker, he has backpacked in Alaska's Denali National Park and Preserve, Wyoming's Grand Teton National Park, and in Great Smoky Mountains National Park. He has completed more than 700 miles of the Appalachian National Scenic Trail.

    Helen Davis is a native of Lewistown, Pennsylvania. She earned a B.S. in Human Ecology from The Ohio State University in 1973, a master's degree in Early Childhood Education from Georgia State University in 1980, and a diploma in Advanced Studies for Teachers from Emory University in 1989. She served as a day care center director, an elementary school educator for twenty-eight years (including twenty years in the Atlanta public school system), and is an Orton-Gillingham-trained reading specialist.

    Ren and Helen are partners in freelance writing and photography, specializing in walking, hiking, and travel. Their most recent works include the fourth edition of *Atlanta Walks: A Comprehensive Guide to Walking, Running and Bicycling the Area's Scenic and Historic Locales* (2011), *Our Mark on This Land: A Guide to the Legacy of the*

◄   *On the trail at Vickery Creek Unit of the CRNRA*

Civilian Conservation Corps in America's Parks (2011*), Atlanta's Oakland Cemetery: An Illustrated History and Guide* (2012, winner of the 2013 Georgia Historical Society's Lilla M. Hawes Award for the most outstanding book on local Georgia history and the 2013 Georgia Writer's Association Authors of the Year award), and *Landscapes for the People: George Alexander Grant, First Chief Photographer of the National Park Service* (2015, winner of the American Library Association INDIEFAB Gold Medal for the most outstanding photography book published in 2015 by an academic or independent press).

Ren and Helen are members of the Atlanta History Center, the Atlanta Preservation Center, the Historic Oakland Foundation, the Atlanta Botanical Garden, the Georgia Appalachian Trail Club, and the Georgia Chapter of the Sierra Club. The couple resides in Brookhaven.